Too Strong to Die

by
Robin Kerl

For my dear Dr. Daniel Resnick of the University of Wisconsin Hospital

My beloved guardian angel, I dedicate this this book to you. A very special heartfelt thank you for saving my life on June 11, 1999. There are no words to express how very much I appreciate all you did for me that day. If I didn't believe in angels before, I certainly do now. God bless you.

"So do not fear, for I am with you; do not be dismayed, for I am your God. I will strengthen you and help you; I will uphold you with my righteous right hand."
Isaiah 41:10

For my dear Dad

Mother and I and your little friend Katy love you and miss you so much. Mom and I are so proud of you for how you dealt with this sickness for the last few years of your life. You were such a fighter--I guess I know whom I get that quality from! I will miss the times we shared together and our talks. Always know that you are loved and will be missed by us all so very much.

1

Forgetting what is behind and straining toward what is ahead, I press on toward the goal to win the prize for which God has called me heavenward in Christ Jesus.

Philippians 3:13-14

Acknowledgements

I first want to thank God for being with me and for saving my life for me on the day that my injury occurred. I can't even put into words how very grateful and thankful I am for everything that the Lord has done for me.

I apologize if I forgot to mention anyone's name. There have been so many people that have been such a blessing to me. I thank all of you so much for everything.

To my loving mom: I know this time is extremely difficult for you with the death of your husband of 45 years. I know that I can't take away the pain and the hurt you are feeling, and I know it feels like a big piece of the puzzle is missing. I will always be available for you to talk to. Mom, thank you for everything. I love you.

To Benjamin Jones, David's father. Ben died on June 1, 2014. I wish you, David, and I could have known each other better. I so wish things didn't end on such a sour note for all of us. I wish that I could have married your son; he was so sweet. I think about the time that you opened up the freezer and found a can of Diet Pepsi I had put in there to get cold. I remember you saying, "Come here and look David, isn't that cute," and you both laughed. It's those times we all shared together that I so wish that I could get back. God bless you, Ben.

I also thank my friend John Smith for everything he does for me.

To my dear beloved grandma Dolores Powers, mom & I miss you so much. It was so hard for us both to let go of you. You were such a strong woman to deal with all the hardship and adversity in your life. I see now just where I got that fighter mentality from! As you often referred to mom & I as your precious angels , your precious angels love you and miss you so much.

Special thanks to two very special friends who have been such a big influence in my life--Pastor Garrett and his wife Lorraine Garrett. You are both a lamp unto my feet and a light unto my path. I cherish the friendship that we share.

I thank my church congregation at Good Shepherd Lutheran Church and all of my pastors there: Pastor Brent Campbell, Pastor Sheryl Ericsson, Pastor Rod Hank, and Pastor Tim Nybroten and Dara Schuller-Hanson. God's peace be with you all.

Thank you Pastor Dara for partnering with me and showing me how to teach Bible study. I can't thank you enough for the opportunity that you have given me to exercise my gifts from God. Your kindness is much appreciated.

Thank you to Pastor Moss, who baptized me the second time back in 2007. We had a very special bond.

Special thanks to my very first pastor, Donald Steven Moss. He was a very special person to me. Little did I know that when I was in the hospital recovering from my broken ankle it would be the very last time that I would ever see him. He was the parking lot attendant at the hospital so he came to my room and said hello when he could. I am so glad he did because about a month after that he died of a stroke. Pastor Moss you will always be in my heart.

Thank you, Pastor Wade, for all of the opportunities that you gave to me to share the word of God with everyone.

To my dear friends Pastor Barry Garrett and Lorraine Garrett who inspired me to write this book. They have both been such a big influence on me in my journey with the Lord. They told me that no matter what the circumstances might look like on the outside to keep on going forward in The Lord. They helped me to believe that I could be a source of strength to them and so many others. I thank you both so very much.

I have so much gratitude for my caregiver, Kim—she is just like a sister to me. I can talk to her about anything.

Thanks to my caretaker Galina and her husband Eugine. Galina you are a very helpful and caring person. I can't thank you enough for everything. Eugene you are so kind; I enjoy talking to you, you have so much wisdom. Thank you both for your friendship. God be with you both.

Thanks to my good friend and caregiver Kim Andraska. Kim, you were such a big help to my family an we all thank you so much for everything. God bless you for the kindness that you showed to all of us.

Thank you to David Meyer, my physical therapist at the University of Wisconsin Hospital in Madison. David touched my heart in a very special way.

Carl Fernandez was one of my physical therapists during my stay at Meriter Hospital when I broke my ankle. Carl you were so very helpful with everything. Has there ever been anyone that has come into your life unexpectedly that you felt a strong connection to you didn't know why? That was the way I felt you with you, Carl. I thank you for all of your help; it was a pleasure to get to know you.

Doctor James R. Bowers was the Doctor on call the night I broke my ankle on Friday December 13. (I was not superstitious before but now I am not so sure now.) I thank you so very much for doing such a great job with my surgery. I am so fortunate you were the doctor on call that night. Thank you Dr. Bowers for your help and your knowledge. "The hand of the Lord was on me, and he brought me out by the Spirit of the Lord and set me in the middle of a valley; it was full of bones. He led me back and forth among them, and I saw a great many bones on the floor of the valley, bones that were very dry. He asked me, 'Son of man, can these bones live?'" Dr. Bowers, if it had not been for your expertise and wisdom my bones would not have lived.

Thank you Doctor Charles Ford who performed surgery on my vocal cords.

Thank you Dr. Donald Mickey. I am so thankful for your help to deal with this most difficult time in my life.

Thank you to my friend Sly, the host of Driving Home with Sly on 93.7.

Thanks, also, to Richard Brown. (Proverbs 27:17 notes, "As iron sharpens iron, so one man sharpens another.")

Thank you to my Support Broker, Brenda Oakes and Self-Employment Coordinator, Shannel Trudeau-Yancey.

Thanks to my book editor, Sheryl Lilke-Cooper.

I thank all of these very special people. Without all of their help this book you are about to read would not have been possible.

Thank you and God bless you all.

Robin

Chapter 1: It's Not Over!

June 11, 1999 was a warm and sunny Friday in Madison, Wisconsin. It started like most days with my fiancé, David, picking me up early to go to Walmart, where we both worked as department managers and where he had recently proposed to me, on one knee, while a group of very surprised co-workers looked on. The moment was captured in a photo that is still displayed in my living room. I was 23 and petite, with a mane of strawberry blond curls; David was 24, burley, and baby-faced. I'll never forget how, after the proposal, one of our friends announced the happy news over the loud speaker so everyone in the store could share in our excitement.

This particular Friday was like any other day. I was looking forward to the upcoming weekend so that I could enjoy time with David. I remember feeling pleased with myself after redecorating my department, Domestics, in a cute duck theme. I called my mom and asked her to come for a visit so I could show off my work, and I also received a few calls from my ex-boyfriend, Jerome, asking me to come out into the parking lot to talk to him. Jerome and I had a history of violence in our relationship. I had successfully put that relationship behind me and was now happily engaged to a kind and loving man, so I ignored his requests and went on with my day. Looking back, even though I wasn't a religious person at the time, I know that God was warning me. I'm glad I listened. We should all learn to listen to that little voice inside us.

One very important discovery I've made in my life is that I deserve much better than to be in a relationship with a violent man. I was able to be on my own and grow stronger and more confident in myself, so that when I met David I was ready to enter into a relationship with a man who expressed his love with great, warm bear hugs instead of with violence. I know now that it's better to be alone than in an awful relationship with a person who abuses you mentally and physically. I made the mistake many time of thinking that Jerome would change. If you find yourself in such a relationship, don't make the same mistake; someone who loves you would never be abusive toward you. Ephesians 5:24 says no one ever hated their own body. God gave you your body; don't let anyone ever mistreat it. If you are in a violent relationship, please find help and get out before something tragic happens; don't learn the hard way like I did. It is difficult to be alone, but sometimes being alone can be the first step to wholeness.

On this particular day David and I finished work at the same time. Before leaving the store we did a little shopping and as we headed out into the bright afternoon sun with our purchases, it seemed like any other beautiful spring day in Madison. There was no indication that Jerome was waiting for us in the parking lot, crouched in the bushes with a gun. Just a few minutes later, David and Jerome would both be dead and I would be lying in a Med-Flight helicopter with a gunshot wound in my head.

At home that afternoon, my rottweiler, T-Bone, was waiting eagerly at the window for David and I to arrive (David kept Milk-bones in his car and gave them to T-Bone so he wouldn't be jealous) while my mom relaxed and watched Oprah. When she heard a news announcer break in to say that there had been an incident at the local Walmart, she turned to the television to see video of the familiar parking lot full of police cars and ambulances. Her mother's intuition told her that something had happened to me and that Jerome had been involved, so she ran across the hall to ask our neighbor, a deputy sheriff, for a ride to Walmart. Unfortunately our neighbor wasn't home, so she drove herself in a daze.

My father was at the bowling alley at the time and when he arrived home, the 911 operator called to tell him to come to Walmart. When my parents both finally arrived I was already gone, taken by MedFlight to the University of Wisconsin Hospital. Police escorted my parents, and David's father, Ben Jones, to the hospital.

At the UW Hospital, a young-looking neurosurgeon told my parents that I was barely alive and that he would have to operate immediately for there to be a chance of saving my life. My mother begged him to not let me die, and he promised to do everything he could. It's very fortunate for me that the gifted Dr. Resnick was on my case that day because, five very long hours later, I was out of surgery and still alive.

That was just the beginning of my struggle to live, however. I went straight from surgery to the ICU where I lay in a coma and on a ventilator. The doctors continued to tell my parents that it was unlikely that I would ever wake up, let alone walk, talk, or even breathe on my own again (God, of course, had a different plan for me). My mom didn't lose hope, however, because the next day as she watched over my terribly injured and unresponsive body, she said to me, "Robin, if you can hear me, squeeze my hand." She says that she felt me squeeze with all my strength. While it was my had squeezing my mother's, it was God's strength that made it move.

When I look back at my long recovery process I see it as the story of how God's love and the love and support of my family and medical team gave me the strength to overcome obstacles and heal wounds. My journey of faith began at the same time as my journey of recovery, and that is the story I want to tell. I believe that I could have never made it though these many years of recovery without this faith. Isaiah, 41:10 says, "Fear not, for I am with thee. Be not dismayed, for I am thy God. I will strengthen thee, yea I will help thee, yea I will uphold thee with the right hand of my righteousness." God was with me, and he gave me strength. When the work I needed to do to eat, talk, and walk seemed too difficult, I just reminded myself that nothing is too difficult for God -- he did raise Lazarus from the dead, after all.

In Proverbs 3:5-7 it says, "In all thy ways acknowledge Him and He shall direct thy path." I have heard it said that when you praise God in every circumstance, your praise not only benefits God, but it also benefits you. That is true because it shows Him that you can praise Him in any situation in your life, be it good or bad. I believe that God has been by my side throughout my life, in both the good times and the bad, in every difficult situation and all of the amazing successes that he has helped me with. I believe that He can do the same for you.

When you have walked through the valley of the shadow of death, people want to hear your words of encouragement, and you want to share your story of survival. I myself have walked through the valley of the shadow of death, and I want to share this story with you. I believe that if God can perform a miracle for me, He can perform one for you too. No matter what challenges life hands you, there is always room for a comeback. I'm living proof of that.

Chapter 2: Trials and Transformation

I was in a coma for about two months. My family was at my bedside every day, and though I would sometimes appear to respond to things happening in the room, I was never fully conscious. My mom remembers that one day my friend Sean was visiting and told me that when I woke up we'd "go out for a beverage" (a private joke between the two of us) and I laughed!

Otherwise I was almost completely non-responsive for these months. At the end, as I was beginning to regain consciousness, I would frequently get very agitated, and flail my body around violently. It was disturbing for my family to see, but the doctors reassured them that it was normal behavior for someone emerging from a coma.

I do have one memory from this time--a vision, maybe, or an out-of-body experience. I remember feeling as if was walking outside on a foggy morning. As I walked along, I saw a figure in the distance. It seemed to be a man, and as I approached he held out his hand as if telling me to stop, like a crossing guard might do. I know now that it was God telling me that it wasn't my time to die because my family needed me. He didn't want me to cross over just yet.

I now believe that this trial that I faced came so that my faith could be strengthened. The way to purify gold is to put it through an extremely hot fire. It is the same way with us. We are put into the fire of adversity so that we also are refined and purified. When we come out of the fire, we are a totally different person. We come out with great substance. I can testify to that, and if you have ever been put through the fire in your own life, you know just what I mean.

Think of a water hose--if you want to see how far the hose can shoot water, you apply pressure to it. The harder you squeeze the nozzle, the further it shoots out water. The same goes for us. The harder and longer we are squeezed, the more our patience and our faith are squeezed. We come to the conclusion in our minds that the strength and help we need can only come from God, and God alone. "What was meant for evil, God used for good" (Genesis 50:20).

I woke up in late August, soon after my 24th birthday. I have very few memories from this time, so my mom has helped me piece together the story of those first few months. I gradually become more and more alert, though I wasn't able to talk or eat or even use my own hands to do simple things like pull the blankets over myself in bed. My mom had to tuck me in each night before she went home. One day my grandmother was by my bedside and my mom called to check in. My grandmother held the phone to my ear so I could hear my mom's voice, and to her surprise she heard me say "Hello!" It was my first word in months and it was music to my mom's ears.

I spent two more months in the hospital before going to a rehab facility. My family was with me every day. I remember not wanting my mom to ever leave my side, not even to go down to the hospital cafeteria for dinner, so she stayed by my side and my grandmother brought her food to the room.

As soon as I was alert the physical therapy started. I had

many therapists, but one that really stands out in my memory was named Dave. Whenever Dave was my therapist I knew it would be a challenging day! Even before I could hold my own weight he wanted me to make the motions of walking. None of us know at the time that it would take years before I could finally walk again, but I knew in my heart that I would some day and Dave's help and encouragement gave me strength and confidence.

I want to touch on the subject of ADLs, better known to many as Activities of Daily Living. They are simple but important tasks like washing your face and brushing your teeth and cooking your meals. For a very long time I could not do any of these things for myself. I needed help with these and so many other things as well--things that we take for granted every day. They might seem minor and irrelevant, but I encourage you to not take it for granted that you can do these things for yourself. I couldn't for a very long time, and I can't even begin to tell you how helpless and inferior that made me feel. It was extremely hard for me when I couldn't walk; I felt kind of ashamed and embarrassed, even though I know now that I shouldn't have.

Another thing that we all take for granted every day is our ability to swallow what we eat and drink. For a very long time after my injury I had to use what is called Thick-It® in all of my drinks except in tomato juice, because that was the consistency that I needed at that time. So much that has changed in my life since that day in June of 1999. I have to be extremely careful how I ration my time, because if I don't take my time and rest in between activities I get awful migraine headaches that can last for two or three days.

I have changed and grown so much over the last years. I have grown so much spiritually; I was not at all religious before I faced these challenges. I now see things in a whole different way than I once did. Coming as close to death as I did changed my whole way of thinking about life. The things that once seemed important to me don't seem as important as they once did. I have much bigger goals in my life that I want to fulfill and bring to fruition. My desire, God be willing of course, is to be active in the ministry. Doing what, I don't quite know yet, but in God's time I know He will reveal that to me.

Thanks be to God for all He has done for me! I am still standing, but I almost was not before God intervened in my situation. A scripture from the Bible that comes to mind comes from 2nd Corinthians 12: 9-10: "My grace is sufficient for you, for my power is made perfect in your weakness." I think of the story in the Bible of Shadrach, Meshach, and Abednego and how they were put in the fiery furnace. They came out of the fire not even smelling like smoke. Yes, there are some of us, myself included, who smell like smoke, but your strength and your miracle is never in what you lost, it's always in what you have left after the fire stops burning. You might be a little burnt, but give thanks to God that you were not destroyed totally.

These first months of my recovery were the most difficult days of my life. So many people thought that I would never talk again, or feed myself, or walk. I was used to being underestimated, though. When I was first promoted to department manager at Walmart, many people thought I couldn't do the job because I was the youngest manager in the store. I proved them wrong and went on to do a great job in my department.

For a while even my mom thought I'd never walk again. There are some things that only a person knows about themselves. I knew in my heart that I'd walk, just as I knew I'd be a great department manager. I know now that God was with me on those difficult days, and with his strength and my own belief in myself I began the long journey of recovery.

1 Thessalonians 5:16 tells us to "be joyful always, pray continually, give thanks in all circumstances, for this is God's will for you in Christ Jesus." Yes, we will all face battles in our lives, but it is how we choose to handle them that makes all the difference in the

14

world—we can sit around and feel sorry for ourselves, or we can work hard to change the situation. I know that I can't change what happened in my past, but I can change my future, and so can you.

I have been through so much, not only since I was shot, but even before then at the hands of my ex-boyfriend. I was physically and emotionally abused by him. When I met David and got engaged to him, I thought to myself that my life was finally starting to get better, that things were finally starting to work out for the good, and that was just when things got much worse. But maybe, now that I think back, the circumstances that I encountered were working on my behalf, although I didn't realize it at the time. They say God works in mysterious ways.

Most of us at one time or another in life will go through the fire of affliction. The purpose of fire and afflictions in our lives is to test our faith. It is easy for us to say we trust God, but it is another to really put what we say into action when everything in our life is turned upside down. Where you are is not as important to God as who you are. I once heard someone say, "If we are not impressed by our strengths—our talents and our abilities—then we can't be depressed by our weakness and our inabilities." I used to get frustrated with the things I can't do very well yet as a result of the injury that I sustained, but then that "still small voice" spoke to me and God said to me, "Robin you are so fortunate to be alive, the other blessings that I have granted to you are just an added extra bonus that I have bestowed onto you."

I see my situation that I am faced with in life kind of like a game of Go Fish. It's all in the way that I play the cards that I have been dealt. If only life gave us the option, like the game, to go fishing for better cards! Unfortunately life doesn't work that way. I know that I make the most out of what cards I have been dealt, play them to the best of my ability, and trust God to direct every play that I make.

I believe that time does in fact heal all wounds. When I get

15

down I encourage myself by thinking that although I might not be where I need to be, thanks to God I am not where I used to be. I have found from my own personal experience that if you keep a positive attitude, you can achieve so much more.

Looking out the window the other day I noticed that it was extremely windy. The strong wind outside that was blowing is very much like the winds of life--they can be strong, but they very rarely do any permanent damage. The wind just makes resistance come into play more. It's the same way in our life; I truly believe that what doesn't kill us will make us stronger. There is a reason that we go through what we go through in life. It's a lot better for our health and general well-being if we go through our trials and tribulations with a positive attitude in all things. Remember, it takes 43 muscles to frown and only 17 to smile, so turn that frown upside down (a good sense of humor is a great thing to have when life gets rough)!

As I write this and remember all the things God has brought me out of and delivered me from, I thank Him so very much for all He has done for me. Some people might question why I have such strong faith. Well, you would too if you went through all that I went through and lived to tell about it. It's very hard just to re-member all of these things; some parts of me wish I would have never had to endure all of these difficulties. But then I look at how much it has enriched my well-being and I realize that if I hadn't had these experiences, I would never be where I am spiritually. In the Bible Paul says that we ought to rejoice in our sufferings. Mine gave me a whole new outlook on life. I have come to believe that one of the reasons we go through all these difficulties and hard-ships is to prepare us for the place God has for us.

To be completely honest, I wouldn't trade what I have learned along this journey for anything. I would not want to go back to how things were before in my life. After all, in the words of T. D. Jakes, "It's not about the journey; it's about what you learned along the way to where you are going." That's so very true; I have learned so much along my journey, things that I wouldn't trade for anything. No amount of money or material things could ever equal what I have learned. For example, I have learned how to be more patient with people. That is one of the many qualities we should all have with each other, because that is one of God's examples to us that He gives us in the Bible. Ephesians 4:2 tells us to be patient toward one another: "Be completely humble and gentle. Be patient, bearing with one another in love."

I sometimes refer to the trial that I have to deal with as developing my pearl. I once heard Joel Olsteen give a sermon about this subject. He said that when an oyster feeds off the bottom of the ocean, he sometimes gets a grain of sand lodged on the inside of him. This causes him discomfort and he doesn't like it. He rubs and rubs trying to get rid of it, but eventually something priceless is developed in him. It's the same way with us. The problem or hardship that we have to endure in life is developing something in us that is priceless, something that no amount of money could ever purchase for us. So even in the tribulation that you might be facing in life, just remember that God will pay you back double whatever you lost. I myself have seen the benefit of loss in my life. I might have lost the man I was going to marry and have a family with, but I have gained so much as a result of this happening in my life.

Yes, many things have happened in my life that I don't understand. When I begin to have questions I remember another thing pastor Joel Osteen said: "Don't put a question mark where God put a period." If God put a period somewhere in your life, just move on, because when God closes one door in your life, He will always open up a much bigger and better door for you. We might not understand it at the moment, but we don't have to understand. God just needs us to believe. I had a plan for my life, but God wanted me to go another direction. No matter how uncomfortable or difficult it is for us, we must always follow the path God has set before us in our lives, because God always knows what path is best for us. God tells us in His Word, "I set before you two choices: life and death." Sometimes He will put us in uncomfortable situations in life to help grow and increase in our faith.

Those two months in the hospital after I awoke from the coma were one struggle after another, and there was little relief in sight. God gave me a choice, however, and I chose life. This meant that there would be a lot of hard work ahead of me, but I had faith in myself. Looking back, I know that God had faith in me too.

Chapter 3: Perseverance

There was no relief for me or my family after I awoke from the coma and began therapy. I spent two more months at UW Hospital and then transferred to a rehab facility in Madison. Along with the stress of my injuries and physical limitations and the very difficult work of therapy, my family and I often felt pushed around by the medical system and confused about making the choices that would be most helpful to my recovery.

My mom and dad had to fight to get me into a rehab facility near Madison so that they'd be able to see me every day. She was often worried that I wasn't being treated well when she couldn't be with me. At one point a doctor told us that he felt that the physical therapy wasn't worth the time because he was certain I'd never walk again. LIttle did he know! His negativity just made me more determined. I had been underestimated before at Walmart and I had proved everyone wrong. I had even been born tiny and , so I learned early in life to fight for survival. There was no way I was going to give up even in the face of the most difficult challenge of my life.

Many people want beauty without ashes and crowns without

crosses, but sometimes you have to go through the bad times in life to get to the blessings God has for you. My advice is to do what you can do and trust God to do what you can't do by yourself. I am speaking from experience when I say that He surely will help you with what you can't do by yourself—all you have to do is ask Him. The reason you have not is because you ask not, just like it tells us in the Bible in the book of James.

How do you see your glass in life? Do you see it as being half empty? Or do you view it as being half full? I believe that how you view your current situation will determine your future. It would have been easy for me to give up and quit, because quitting takes little effort. No, I did not get to where I am today overnight. It has been extremely hard for me, but if God can see me through all of my heartache and all of my hurt, He can also see you through yours.

Due to the extent of the injury I sustained when I was shot, I have lost some bodily functions. I can no longer see out of my left eye and I wear a hearing aid in my left ear. This is a great loss but the Bible tells us in Matthew 5:30, "It is profitable for thee that one of the members should perish, and not that the whole body be cast into hell." I know that all this has happened to me for a reason; I just not have completely figured out what God's reason is yet, but as it says in Deuteronomy 29:29, "The secret things belong unto the Lord," so I will just put my faith and confidence in Him and just know that He has everything in control. That's the kind of peace that only God can give unto you and me.

I spent six months at the rehab facility, and they were the toughest months of my life. I had to have physical and occupation-al therapy to learn to use my hands again -- I hand no coordination and my writing and drawing looked like a child's. for five months I was fed through a tummy tube, and had to re-learn to chew and swallow starting with only thick liquids and very soft food. And, of course, the struggle to walk continued. Someone said during this time that they had never seen a patient work as hard as me. Looking back I know that God was giving me strength to keep trying.

For the first few months, my mom made sure that I didn't learn the details of the shooting. Before every therapy session and doctor appointment she quietly reminded everyone to not let the truth slip out because she wanted me to be strong enough to hear the news. She would know when the time was right. So until November I was just told that there had been a bad accident. My mother spoke to a psychologist about the best way to share the truth with me, and she was sick to her stomach when the day finally arrived. I have to say that I was not very surprised to learn that I had been shot by Jerome, though it was very hard to hear that David had died. My mom says that I just listened to the news quietly, and she reassured me that while David was dead, I was alive and that he would want the best for me. I knew I had to press on and move forward with my life to honor him.

We have all heard the song from the movie The Titanic. The song has a very meaningful name for me: "My Heart Will Go On." I also must have the courage and the will to go on. It is so very hard for me to press on after all that has happened to me. After losing the man I thought I would spend the rest of my life with, I have had to start all over learning things as little children do, but it has given me a whole new perspective and outlook on life that I did not have before. So if you have had unfortunate things happen to you in your life, instead of thinking how the situation has worked against you, turn it around and try to discover how it has worked for your benefit. That is what I must do quite frequently. That's just one of the many tricks the devil plays on us--he tries to discourage us and distort our thinking about just how bad things look so that we lose our focus.

As the Bible shows us in the book of Nehemiah, if you have been or are in the process of experiencing trouble or trials in your life, you just might have to rebuild your wall as they did also in the

Bible. Through all of the trials and tribulations that I am experiencing, I also have had to rebuild my wall, not just in one aspect of my life, but in every way that you can imagine. I might not be working at a job, but I consider myself to be working for the Lord in a spiritual sense. Ministry is not a 9 to 5 job, but rather one that has you on call seven days a week and 24 hours a day. Sometimes I will get an idea in the middle of the night and have to arise out of a sound sleep to write it down. My sleep might be interrupted, but I see that as just how the chips fall. That's the best time; the time when God can communicate with us. That's the time when our minds are not preoccupied with the daily grind of life. So like the Bible says in the book of James, Chapter 1, "Consider it pure joy, my brothers, whenever you face trials of many kinds, because you know that the testing of your faith develops perseverance. Perseverance must finish its work so that you may be mature and complete, not lacking anything."

Just as the Bible tells us in Philippians, stay focused on the prize that's ahead of you, no matter what the circumstances might look like in the natural realm. Because we must first obtain it in the spiritual sense before it can manifest in the natural world that we live in. I know in my heart that if I hadn't been so diligent and persistent in my recovery, I wouldn't be where I am today.

We have all heard the saying, "If at first you don't succeed, try again." To this day those words still ring true in my heart. I have fallen many times in trying to regain all that I lost when I was hurt, but if I can make it through all that I have, so can you, no matter what you are going through in your life. Just be patient and try as best as you can to take it one day at a time. I know from personal experience that it's very hard, but just remember where you were at one time in your life and take a look at all God has brought you through. The battles that you are facing in life do not belong to you, they belong to the Lord.

I was thinking one day to myself, Why must I endure all this hardship and heartache? But then I was doing my Bible study reading and I came across this scripture in the Bible, from John 9:1-7, where Jesus says, "Neither hath this man sinned nor his parents; it has come about so that the works of God should be made manifest in him." My question as to why was then answered.

I don't mean to brag, but I know a lot of people wouldn't even have the strength or the tenacity to go through all that I went through in life. Many people in my position would have given up and quit a long time ago. We all have days when we are discouraged and wish that our recovery was coming along faster than it was. Today, as I am writing, is one of those days. Do ever just feel like throwing in the towel and not having to go through whatever you are going through? I know that I should not feel this way, because God has brought me from a very mighty long way, but there are times when I just don't want to do this anymore. I know that how far I have come only brings honor to God's name, and that is what I most want to do—bring honor and glory to His name. That's why I persevere.

Some of you may feel that you are under the attack from an enemy and you don't know why. I also am facing this persecution from the enemy in going about my daily activities. Now that I think about it, it has become so very clear to me as to why this is happening to me. The devil isn't fighting me so hard because of where I am right now, but because of where I am going on my journey with the Lord. So if you also are enduring hardship and persecution in your life, that is why.

Maybe this can help us appreciate the hardships we face, even though the struggle can be very tiresome. We have all at one time seen race horses with blinders on their face to help them focus their gaze straight ahead of them. We sometimes have to do the same exact thing in life so that we can keep our eyes fixed on the prize ahead of us. It's very easy to lose sight of your main goal in life, and there will be many things that try to get you to lose focus on your God-given destiny. The desires and the cravings of the flesh can be very distracting, but God will provide a way out for us. The Bible tells us in 1st Corinthians 10:13, "No temptation has overtaken you except what is common to mankind. And God is faithful; He will not let you be tempted beyond what you can bear. But when you are tempted, He will also provide a way out so that you can endure it."

This Bible verse speaks to my heart personally when I read it: "For I know the plans I have for you, declares the Lord, plans to prosper you and not to harm you, plans to give you hope and a future" (Jeremiah 29:11). When those feelings of doubt and insecurity come, just remember the situation that you were once in that God has delivered you out of. Try thinking back to where you once were at one time in your life and look at where you are now right, and thank God for how far He has brought you. I think of the book of Job in the Bible. My life has been much like his; I also lost everything all at once like Job did--my health, my fiance. Job said to his wife, "Shall we accept the good from God, and not trouble?" That is so very true, because in Romans 5: 3-4 the Bible tells us so plainly that our suffering produces perseverance, and character, and also hope.

Joyce Meyer said, "I might not have had a good start in life, but I plan on having a dynamic finish in life." I had a very bad hand of cards dealt to me in the first part of my life, but I plan to turn that all around in my life for the second half, and if you didn't have a good first part of your life you also can turn that around. Pastor David Jeremiah said once on his radio broadcast: "You can expect failure as a fact of life, but don't expect it as a way of life." If I would have quit every time I failed, I wouldn't have won the prize that was set before me, and neither will you if you quit. I again remember Philippians 3:12: "Not that I have already obtained all this or have already been made perfect, but I press to take hold of that for which Christ took hold of me."

Chapter 4: Overcoming Limitations

There are no limits in your life when you have God with you. With God all things are possible, if you just call on His name. Looking back at where I was in the first months after the shooting and seeing how far God has brought me, I know that what they say is true—when you have been through the fire and conquered it, you never look at things the same way. I now see life's challenges in a whole different light then I did before all of this happened to me. In started as a physical journey, but it ended up being a spiritual journey as well. I never in a million years could have ever dreamed I would be where I am now, both spiritually and physically.

I was able to move back home in March, nine months after the shooting. Life still consisted almost entirely of rehab, with in-home aids and at various facilities in the Madison area. Though I was still learning to swallow, write, and perform other activities of daily living, what I focused on most was walking. For the next few years that was the most important thing in my life. Whenever somebody asked me what my goals for the future were, I had only one answer: To walk.

As a result of the gunshot wound itself and the tubes that

helped me breathe while I was in a coma, swallowing was especially difficult for me and my voice was very hard to understand. A wonderful surgeon, Dr. Ford, performed surgery on my throat and vocal chords that changed everything. I am so very thankful that eating and drinking became much easier for me. When I saw Dr. Ford after the surgery, I gave him a big hug and told him how his work had improved my life. He replied with a smile, "That's what being a doctor is all about!" Dr. Ford was one of many angels watching over me, and I am so grateful that I was able to have my surgery performed by him just before he retired.

One thing I learned from this experience is the power of focusing on the truly important things in life. It can be easy to get caught up in things that don't really matter, but when we stop and refocus our attention on what really matters the most in life, we can accomplish great things. The Bible tells us in 2 Corinthians 4:18, "What is seen is temporary, but that which is unseen is eternal." It's very easy to set your mind on the small events of today, but we must remember to also think about what really matters the most: where you will spend eternity. When I think about everything that I have had to relearn and endure I realize that if I was not up to this challenge, God would not have brought this across my path. But I am more than a conqueror. I can do all things through Christ who gives me strength (Philippians 4:13).

I didn't feel like a conqueror every day. Rehab went on and on, and after two years I still wasn't walking. The repetition was especially difficult -- the same exercises, over and over, day after day. I think many people would have given up, but it's just not in me to accept failure. At the end of the two years one doctor, Dr. Ebert, said that it was time to end formal rehab because it was obvious that I'd never walk. Well, as you can imagine, Dr. Ebert's negative attitude just made me try even harder to reagin everything that I had lost. In fact, I think it was the exact motivation I needed at the time, and obviously God had plans for me to be an exception to the rule. So I say good-heartedly to Dr. Ebert, thank you for your lack of encouragement; it was just what I needed!

I encourage you to never put a limit on what you can do in your life; God doesn't use perfect people for His work. He uses imperfect people for His glory, so that we can see that along with our own power and strength, we also need God to work through us. Look at Peter in the Bible—he had many flaws in his personality, but God still worked through him. God is not looking for perfect people; He is looking for people who are willing to work with him. Your attitude about yourself should be, "I am no better than anyone else, but I am no worse than anyone else, either." Maybe up until now your life has gone very well, but speaking to you from personal experience, I urge you not to judge the second half of your life by the first half. As the Bible says in Job 8:7, "Though the beginning was small, yet the later end should greatly increase." I expect a great second half of my life, even though much of the first half was not so good.

Human nature has a tendency toward doubt or disbelief. We should believe what God has said in His Word to us. A scripture from the Bible that comes out of Mark 9:24 says, "Lord I believe; help my unbelief." If I would have harbored unbelief in my heart as to the exceeding greatness of God's power to do exceedingly above all that anyone can ever think or imagine (Ephesians 3:20-21), I would not be where I am today in my life. I know that I have not yet reached my full potential, but thank God I am not where I used to be. I realize that I have a ways to go yet in my recovery and my spiritual development, but when I think back about all that I have overcome I rejoice even more greatly in the Lord and give all the credit and thanks to Him.

Joel Osteen's wife, Victoria, said, "If you want to change your life, change your thoughts." How we see our future helps to determine it. Create a picture in your head of what direction you want your life to go in, and every time those thoughts of defeat

27

from the devil tell you that you can't, think to yourself: Yes, I can.

That's what I had to do after my two years of physical therapy ended. I pictured myself walking, and that's what I set out to do. Because some people thought it wasn't worth it to continue to try, my family and I had to fight to get what I needed to continue striving toward my goal. Though there was no longer hospital-based physical therapy, I was given a membership at the gym in the University of Wisconsin sports medicine center where I could get help from people on staff. I was determined to be an exception to the rule, just as I have been as a premature baby and a young department manager.

Isn't it interesting how different people can be in the same situation and have very different opinions of the matter at hand? In the Bible in Numbers 13:30-31, when Joshua and Caleb and ten others returned from spying out the Promised Land, the others said, "We don't stand a chance." Caleb, however, said, "No problem, we can do this." If you set your mind to thinking that something is too difficult, then you'll never accomplish it. Instead, try to have a mindset like Caleb did. Believe that you can. In my own situation, I know that a lot of people would see this circumstance as impossible to overcome, but I choose to view it as a minor setback in my life on my way to my Promised Land. We can either view obstacles as impossible to overcome or we can simply view them as temporary setbacks. It's kind of like climbing a ladder -- just take it one rung at a time.

When the two years of rehab had ended, it would have been so very easy for me to quit and give up. But quitting does not take any effort. It takes effort to preserve and push through the problem. Trials in the end strengthen us. They show us just what we are really made of. I always knew I was a strong-willed person, but this trial that I am facing confirms that. So when trials come don't despise them, as most people do, but learn to embrace them, as odd as that may sound.

Here is an idea I heard. Picture your mind as an alarm clock that you must set for a certain time. You might have a dream in your life, as I do, that you want to achieve and bring to pass. You must first make up your mind that you are going to achieve that dream no matter what the devil throws at you, because raising obstacles is one of the many tricks he has to try and steal the dream God has placed within you. He knows that if he can abort the dream, then he won't have anything to worry about. So no matter what the dream might be, always keep it in the front of your mind. Don't let the devil distract you from the destination God wants you to travel toward.

So I continued to work, almost every day, at home and at the gym to gain back my strength and endurance. Sometimes, if I needed extra help, a good family friend and church deacon named John who had often visited me in the hospital would come to the gym with me to hold me up while I practiced standing. One caregiver who worked with me at home, Kim, was especially helpful and encouraging. Many other people sent to me by the agency couldn't be depended on to really help. Many of them thought it was too much work, or too boring and repetitive, or not worth it, to help me with my goal to walk. During times of crisis we really learns who is on our side and who isn't.

We must have faith that we can conquer any hardship in life that comes our way; without God's help, everything is impossible. If I can conquer the adversities that I faced in my life, you can do the same thing. Life is not always easy, but I think of it as being like delayed gratification. When you do overcome whatever your obstacle is, you will look back and know that you have done something that you once thought was impossible.

We get to choose whether to have a positive or negative outlook on life. It's easy to have self-pity and ask, "Why me?" In the words of David Jeremiah, "Why NOT you?" I don't know about you, but I wonder to myself why some people think that they are too good of a person to be tested. Jesus himself was even put to the test and tempted by the devil—in Matthew 4:3 the devil said to Jesus, "If you are the Son of God, command these stones be made bread." Notice the devil tried to trap Jesus a total of three different times, and every single time the devil tried to trap Him, Jesus quoted scripture to back up His words. We should follow the example Jesus set for us. We should be able to back up the words that we say to others with scripture. I have found that when we are able to quote directly from the Bible, it adds an element of surprise to the conversation that we are engaged in with the other person.

It would have been so very easy for me to settle and just stay where I was after I was hurt. I could have said, Well, I can't walk and I can't talk very well, but this is good enough, at least I'm alive" I couldn't just settle for good enough though. That's just not the kind of person I am. I don't believe in doing just enough to get by. The Bible tells us to go above and beyond in everything. There will always be two voices in your head—the first one will tell you that you have already reached your God-given potential, but the second voice will tell you that you are meant for more, that there are no limits on your life. You can do anything. The Creator of the universe breathed his life into you, so don't put limits on yourself. If God hasn't, then you shouldn't either. I never thought that I could ever do and accomplish all that I have, but with God's help I have. As it says in the Bible in Philippians 4:13, "I can do everything through Christ who gives me strength." So put your hope and trust in God.

My friend Kris used to call me The Dancing Queen. I was determined, at the very least, to earn the name of The Walking Queen at some point in the future. Walking become my single focus in life, the only goal I would consider. I even resisted other types of therapies and refused to consider the opinions of many people, even Dr. Ebert, who believed I would never walk on my own again. Dr. Ebert must not have known that with God on my side, anything was possible!

Kim was such a kind and determined caregiver that my mom eventually hired her to care for me full time. Other caregivers had given up or tired out, but not Kim. Together we practiced and practiced. Several years later my mother ran into Lydina, a caregiver who had worked with me for a while, at the store where she worked. Lydina was telling my mom about her new baby and how difficult it was to find good care for her. Like any mother, she only wanted the best for her baby. "Funny how everything seems different when it's your own child, doesn't it," my mom said to her. Many of the caregivers assigned to me by the agency thought my mom and dad were difficult to work with, but the truth is they believed in me and, like all parents, they wanted the best for their child.

Fortunately, Kim and I never gave up. Six years after the shooting--four entire years after most people had given up hope--I took my first steps! It was a Saturday morning, and I was in my bedroom after breakfast doing my daily balance exercises when I took a few steps on my own just as Dr. Resnick said I eventually would. In all of the six years of re-learning how to do everything--talking, swallowing, writing--this was by far the biggest victory. Though I knew I still had a long road ahead of me, I was finally on my way to being The Walking Queen!

In life, growing and learning is a process. I am still going through the process of relearning everything that I once knew how to do. Unfortunately, I had to retrain my brain so much more than the average person does in life. The process is a lot like baking a cake. First you need all the ingredients, and then you need to follow the recipe. If you skip an ingredient the thing that you are baking will taste funny. In the very same way, if we skip an ingredient we will also be lacking as individuals. It might seem like it's saving you time, but in the long run you will not receive the full benefit of baking the recipe as it was intended. Sometimes I wish I could subtract things from all that I must relearn but I know that later

31

on I would regret it. If you have the urge to skip a step in life, just remember and take this advice from someone who has been there: In the end you don't want to think to yourself, "I had the opportunity to learn something, but I skipped that very important step." We often want to go to the next level before we are ready, but to truly overcome we must be patient and know that God's timing is perfect in every situation.

Speaking of my own personal life, I desire to preach God's most Holy Word, but deep down in my heart I know that I am not ready; there is so much more for me to learn yet. Isaiah 46:10 tells us that God makes known "the end from the beginning." I am not sure what my end will be, but I just know in my spirit that God has something GREAT in store for me, so I will just continue to put my faith and trust in God and know that eventually all he has in store for me will come to fruition, and that no weapon formed against me shall prosper.

Chapter 5: Priorities

In the summer of 2007, once my recovery was well underway, John, the family friend and church deacon who often helped me practice walking, invited me to join him and his wife, Geneva, at Bible study. Although I believed in god, my family had never been very religious. One Sunday morning I accompanied him to church services and I like it very much. I immediately felt at home among all the other believers and God's house soon became a place of safety and comfort for me. Being a part of the new community and learning to accept God's word into my heart was such a healing experience for me that I soon made the decision to became baptized (although I had been baptized as a baby, this time had a new meaning for me). I've been attending church every Sunday since that first time.

When we accept Jesus into our life and heart we are reborn. The Bible says in 2 Corinthians 5:17, "Therefore if anyone is in Christ, he is a new creation. The old has gone, the new has come. All this is from God, who reconciled us to himself through Christ, and gave us the ministry of reconciliation." Being alone with God is the first step toward wholeness. When I began my religious studies I soon discovered that reading the Bible and spending time alone with God helped me to accomplish so much more than I ever could without him. I also found that it became easier for me to slow down and enjoy the journey that I am on. My philosophy in life now is to try to enjoy where I am on the way to where I am going.

I once heard Joyce Meyer say, "Enjoy where you are at on the way to where you are going." We get so caught up in thinking about what we will be doing in our future that we tend to forget to live in the present. Take animals for example—they live in the present moment they are in; they don't worry about what is to come. In the Bible in Matthew 6:25, God's Word so plainly tells us not to worry! Yet for some reason we all do anyway, thinking that worrying will resolve or help matters, when in fact it often makes matters worse. Too much worrying can even result in health problems. The cure is to surrender your problems to God. As the Bible tells us in 1 Peter 5:7, "Cast all your cares on Him," because He cares for you. Many of us feel that a person is not working hard in every single moment, then they are wasting time. It might just be that they are preparing themselves for tomorrow. The Bible tells us in Joshua 3:5, "Consecrate yourself for tomorrow."

It was very hard for me at first to understand God's Word to us, but as I applied myself to read some of the Bible every day, I began to understand it better. I soon found some passages that spoke directly to my heart, including the Psalm that begins, "The Lord is my shepherd, I shall not want." And, of course, I immediately felt a kinship with David the shepherd boy. Everyone doubted his ability to defeat the giant, but he came out victorious, just as I had.

I continue to attend a weekly Bible study that has given me a clearer understanding of God's Word. A verse in the Bible, 2 Timothy 2:15, tells us to "study to show thyself approved unto God." In order to truly know and keep all of God's commands, we must study. The Bible tells us in Proverbs 6:21, "Bind them continually upon thine heart and tie them about thy neck." In Mark 9:24 at the end of the verse the father of a boy possessed by demons says, "LORD I believe, help Thou me with my unbelief." I can identify with that statement extremely well, because before I went through this fire of affliction, I believed in God and in heaven, but not as strongly as I do now. In kingdom principals, we are to believe first and then we see the results, but the earthly realm tells us that only if see it physically can we believe. Just as we all want our own children to believe is us, as their parents, God the father wants us to believe in Him. Kingdom principals and our ways are much different. It took me a long time to get my mind thinking according to kingdom principals rather than in the earthly way I was accustomed to.

In the book of Romans the Bible tells us, "Do not conform any longer to the pattern of this world, but be transformed by the renewing of your mind." I had to do that with a lot of things in my life—in other words, I had to put things and priorities in my life in proper order. People prioritize in their lives without even knowing it; whatever you devote your time in life to, that is what you are most interested in. If you devote most of your time and energy into making money, that is what you are most interested in. But how many of us have heard the phrase, "You can't take it with you"? In the book of Matthew 6:24, Jesus says, "No one can serve two masters. Either he will hate the one and love the other, or he will be devoted to one and despise the other. You cannot serve both God and money at the same time." Everything that we have comes from God to begin with; we are just stewards of the money and treasures He has entrusted to us. Think of it like this: We are His personal bankers, who are just holding it for Him until He comes back to get us before the Rapture.

The Bible says that when we get to heaven we will all be rewarded with crowns by God for being faithful to Him. I don't know what you all intend to do with the crowns you receive from God, but I intend to give mine right back to Him as a way to thank Him for all He has done for me. I have that yearning in me to be able to give something back to Him as a way to say thank you for all He has done for me. I know that right now I can give God my time and talents, which I do every day. Every morning I give Him the very first part of my morning. When I spend the first few hours of my day with God, I find that my day goes much more smoothly and I am able to do my best work. My pastor often says that if we do anything in a sloppy way, it is of no benefit to us. Do everything unto the Lord and knowing you shall reap a harvest if you faint not.

One of the many things that I have learned from my experience of almost dying is that you are never promised that you will live to see tomorrow. My advice is to do you very best at everything you do, because you never know, the day that you are currently living just might be your very last day here on Earth. Even if everyone else isn't aware that you're giving your very best effort, God knows, and He knows your heart, and He knows whether you gave it your very best or not.

I feel that I spent a lot of time in the past doing frivolous things, going from one thing to another. I denied God first place in my life. Many of these meaningless, frivolous things will not be of any benefit to me in the future. Based on my experience, I urge you to not waste a day of the life that God has blessed you with. Don't be careless, like I was, with the time that God has given you. Make the most of every day, because every day is a gift from God.

I often ask myself if it is okay that I possess different values than most people? I devote most of my free time to studying God's most holy Word, by either reading and studying or watching church programs on television. People might wonder why I devote so much of my free time to God's Word. The truth of the matter is it just makes me feel so good, like I am actually investing my time in something important, rather than wasting it on things that don't matter. Many people just live and do things for that day, but I want my days and time to be an investment for the future days that are before me.

The days that are given to us are a gift, and we should be interested in others' well-being too. Not just the selfish three of us—me, myself, and I. In the Bible, when the Lord asked Cain, "Where is Abel?" Cain replied, "Am I my brother's keeper?" YES, the truth is we are all our brothers' and sisters' keepers. As Aretha Franklin's sang, every person deserves R-E-S-P-E-C-T! We don't have to like everyone, but we are commanded by Jesus to love one another. This can be quite difficult, because our instinct sometimes is the opposite, telling us to get even with those who have wronged us. This is extremely hard for me, ever since I was hurt. The Bible tells us in Luke 6:29, "If someone strikes you on one cheek, turn to him the other also."

That is why I meditate on God's Word every day—I want to learn his way of thinking. In Psalm 1 the Bible tells us, "Blessed is the man" whose "delight is in the Law of the Lord, and on his Law he meditates day and night." It is very important to understand how our loved ones think and to not jut know of God, but to know Him personally and intimately for yourself.

The letters B. I. B. L. E. stand for "Basic Instruction Before Leaving Earth." I have this saying printed on my computer mouse pad. It keeps my mind focused on what I should be thinking about. If I didn't have that saying in front of me, I might be tempted to focus my attention on carnal thoughts. It's so very easy for you and me to walk by what the flesh wants and desires, but we all must learn to walk by the Spirit instead. In Romans 7:15 Paul says, "I do not understand what I do. For what I want to do I do not do, but what I hate I do." I'm sure all of us can relate to that statement every now and then! I know I do!

Ponder this thought: A wedding ring symbolizes marriage

and that you belong to another, correct? In the same way, baptism represents that we belong to Christ. When we are baptized we are buried with him in death so that then we might be raised with him in new life. After your wedding day and your honeymoon are over, you spend time getting to know your new spouse, yes? In the same way, our desire should be to get to know and spend personal and intimate time with God; he is our new spouse and best friend.

I believe that there is a difference between having a religion with God and a relationship with God. Ask yourself, in your heart, "Am I just dating God on Sundays, or am I married to him?" If you are married to him, involve him in every part of your life--not just in some parts of your life on certain days, but in every day of your life, because after all God grants us every day that is given to us. A Cher song that I love called "I Found Someone" comes to mind -- our relationship to Jesus is that way. When we find and put our trust in Jesus as our personal friend and savior we have indeed found someone to take away all of the heartache and all of the pain that has been inflicted to us in our life.

Don't make the mistake of putting God's will last place in your life. Don't use God and prayer as just an occasional substitute for the real thing. There is every kind of substitute imaginable these days -- sweeteners, creamers -- but there is no substitute for the one true living God. God created us with a special place in our hearts meant just for Him, and until He is at home there we won't experience or have any peace whatsoever. We can try to stuff everything imaginable in that space, but nothing will ever be complete until God is at home there.

I think of St. Augustine's saying, "Our heart is restless until it rests in you, oh Lord." Until I came to know God for myself in a personal way, I didn't experience any peace in my life at all. It is one thing to know about God, but it is a whole different thing to know Him personally and be able to call upon Him as a friend in any situation in your life. The Bible tells us in 2 Corinthians 4:17

that "our light and momentary troubles are achieving for us an eternal glory that far outweighs them all. So we fix our eyes not on what is seen, but what is unseen, since what is seen is temporary, but what is unseen is eternal."

If you learn only one thing from my story, remember this: You can never replay a certain moment in your life. With all the technology that we have these days is seems easy to rewind. In life it's not that easy though. If only it were, life would not pass us by so quickly. Make the most of every moment God has granted you. Oh, how I wish that I didn't have to find that out the hard way.

I compare our life and the path we are on in life to that of a train track. Sometimes in life's many twists and turns we may get derailed and lose sight of what God intends for us to focus our energy on. I know that some times in my own personal life I have, and God has to stop me and get me back into a proper perspective about my situation. Take Jonah in the Bible, for instance. He needed to get his perspective back in life, and God provided the time for him in the belly of a great whale.

How many times do we say, "I just don't have time?" Maybe God arranges it that way on purpose, so that He can see what we devote our free time to. Just a thought! If we say, "I would study more and pray more if I had the time," and if God then gives us that time and we fail to do so, it doesn't make us look so good in the eyes of God, does it? No matter how busy we are, there's always time in the schedule for God. In fact, everything else in life runs more smoothly when we save time for Him. The Bible tells us to choose between life and death. What we choose to do in our free time does make a difference. Even if it seems insignificant to you and I, God knows exactly what you spend your free time on.

You might want to try living your life by the statement, "Discipline is doing what needs to be done when it needs to be done, and doing it that way every time that you do it." I am tempted at times to do otherwise and be unproductive in my own life, but I would not have reached even one of the many goals of my goals in life if I would have just lived for the day at hand and just submitted and pleased my flesh. I try my very best every day to do the will of the Spirit of God and not submit my own desires. Please don't misunderstand me: I am not saying it's easy, because it's extremely hard for anyone to do. That's why the book of Romans 12: 2 tells us, "Do not conform to the pattern of this world, but be transformed by the renewing of you mind." As Paul said in the book of Philippians 3:12-14, "Not that I have already obtained all this, or have arrived at my goal, but I press on to take hold of that for which Christ took hold of me. Brothers and sisters, I do not consider myself to have taken hold of it, but one thing I do, forgetting what is behind and straining toward what is ahead, I press on toward the goal to which God has called me heavenward in Christ Jesus." I realize I have a ways to go yet in my spiritual walk with the Lord, but I have this deep desire in me to do His work. In light of all His great and many wonderful works He has done for me, I just want to somehow repay Him. It's a feeling that is difficult to describe; maybe you feel the same way. I am just so very grateful for everything he has blessed me with.

So, we must stay focused. Just as we keep our camera lens clean, we must also keep our lens clean. If we don't, it will skew our perception. Ever since I joined the church and began studying God's word, I have been able to maintain my focus on what is important in life: God, family, friends. I am speaking from my heart when I tell you that there is going to come a time in your life when you long for the time that you once had with the people that meant so much to you. Don't get upset with the people you love over small things. Slow down and enjoy the journey. We rush through life and take for granted all of the small things as well as the people who mean so very much to us. We never stop and think about how it will be when we no longer have those people in our lives. Please take this advice from someone who lost the person she was going to marry and have a family with: One day we will see that the trivial things in our lives that we view as important now are comparatively very unimportant. Jesus said in Matthew 6:25, "Take no thought for your life, what ye shall eat or what ye shall drink, nor for your body, what ye shall put on. Is not the life more than meat and the body more than raiment?"

My faith and my church community have done so much for me over the past seven years. I have been given the opportunity to speak at church, and have grown to love delivering words of encouragement to the whole community, even though I was very nervous at first. I am also preparing to lead the Bible study group at my church, a job that will give me the opportunity to share my faith with others as well as deepen my own understanding of God's word. All of this, from a person who was expected to die on that day way back in 1999! Well, with God's strength I've kept my focus and will continue delivering both my story and God's word for as long as I can.

Chapter 6: Others' Opinions

Along your journey, you will meet many people who have their own opinions about how you should be going about things. I have found from my own personal experience that some people just enjoy hearing themselves talk. There are only two people who know for sure what's right for you, however, and those two are you and God. No other opinions really matter.

I'm sure you've heard the expression, "Too many cooks spoil the broth." Similarly, in the Bible the book Song of Solomon 2:15 speaks of "little foxes that spoil the vines." My advice is to not let those little foxes that you meet in life influence the decisions that you make every day. People usually mean well, but you have to be the one to make the final call for your own life. I know if I would have listened to everyone's ideas about how I should do things that I would not be where I am today. Some people might think they know what's best for you but they rarely do. Although I've overcome impossible circumstances, I still have a long journey ahead of me. I am very aware of that, of course, but I thank God for where I am today, and that I am not where I was yesterday. With each day that passes by I know that I am one step closer to my destiny.

There are some people who may want to possess the gifts and talents that you have, but don't want to have to endure the challenges you went through to get where you are. It is common for people to want the perks from God's favor without have to face hardship. It's wrong to envy what another person has when you don't know what they went through to get it. You must first show God what you are made of, and after He sees that, He will bless you beyond belief. You must first make that exchange with Him. If you don't believe me, try going to a store and getting your items without making an exchange of money for the items. The exchange that you make with God might be your time, your money, your talents, or the exchange might be in serving at your church—whatever you decide, there must be an exchange made between you and God.

God has blessed me so abundantly in life with so many blessings. God has kept me in my right mind. It's such a blessing to arise every morning clothed in your right mind. I used to take that for granted, but I don't anymore because I know from personal experience that all I have can be taken away from me in a split second. I am very thankful for the one ear of mine that can hear. Just to be able to speak in another thing I am grateful for. I could go on and on.

One very important lesson I've learned is to not let others be in charge of your happiness. You know yourself, and what your needs are, better than anyone. No other person can fulfill these needs better then you can, so why give others a job that you are capable of doing yourself? We are in charge of our own happiness—not our kids or our spouse or our parents—but we tend to pass off the responsibility to others. In 1 Samuel 30:6 it says, "David encouraged himself in the Lord." That's what we must do also. It's nice to have the approval of family and friends, but most of our encouragement must come from within.

You might think it strange that after everything I've been through, my deepest desire is to repay the Lord for all that He has given to me and done for me. Have you ever been surprised by a deep desire to do something that you never thought would happen? For me, it is a deep desire to do something great for the Lord someday. I know that I seem strange to some, but I think differently than most people. Yes, some people think I'm a little weird. In fact, a very good friend of mine told me that some people see me as being a little bit "off." But I am living my life for eternity, not for the temporal things of this world. A passage in 2 Corinthians 4:18 says, "Fix your eyes not on what is seen, but on what is unseen, for what is seen is temporary, but what is unseen is eternal."

Different people hope for different kinds of blessings. As I write this, Christmas is quickly approaching. If you ask one person what he would like for a gift he might answer a new home, or he might say a vacation. Another person who has health issues might just wish to feel well again. I can identify with that because I would give anything to have my health and well-being restored. A scripture in the Bible that really gives heed to this can be found in the Book of Proverbs 14:10: "Each heart knows its own bitterness, and no one can share in its joy."

I experience a great hunger for God, and maybe you do as well. It is not the physical hunger that we all experience, but a hunger in the soul. The hunger I have can never be fulfilled. The more that I am in God's Word and in His house (the church), the more I want of Him. It's a burning desire that I have in my heart to know as much about God as possible.

Although it is not necessary to always heed the opinion of every person you meet, it is best to put disagreements of opinion aside as much as possible. We might not like everyone we come in contact with, but Jesus said, "Love one another as I have loved you" (John 13:34). Loving the unlovely person is a very hard thing to do, but God's Word commands us to.

Creflo Dollar defines "offended" like this: "To take off and end the process." The devil and his dark forces try their very best to offend us every day, but we must remember what the Bible says about God and the devil in 1 John 4:4, "greater is He who is in you than he who is in the world." Whatever the devil throws at you, always remember this.

The Bible tells us in Matthew 9:17, "Neither do men put new wine into old bottles, else the bottles break and the wine runneth out and the bottles perish, but they put new wine into new bottles and both are preserved." In the same way, we might need to reevaluate the friendships we keep. If the people we associate with act or speak in an ungodly way, then we might need to find some different, more positive people to hang around with. I heard a very true statement about this subject on Joyce Meyer's television broadcast: "We are to be affecting people, and they should not be affecting us." The company we keep reflects on us, so we must choose our company wisely. You might want to ask yourself this question about where your friends go: Would I take Jesus there? If your answer is no, then you should not be going there either (if you are Christian at all times and not just on Sunday morning).

Some people are tempted to settle for mediocrity after experiencing misfortune, but I just can't do that. I have a deep burning desire that God has placed within me to get myself back to where I once was before my health was snatched away from my grasp so unfairly. I believe that "Where there is a will there is a way." So many people said that I would never walk again, or have a normal life. But other people don't have the final say in your life; God has the last word as to what does and doesn't happen. I am so very thankful for the strength that He provides me with each day to make it through. I know that left to my own strength I could not endure this hardship every day. I give God all of praise, honor, glory.

My church bulletin once contained the advice: "Before your

burden overcomes you, you must trust God to put His arms underneath you." I have found this to be true in my own life. I have won many battles, but I am aware that the war isn't over. As the song goes, "we have only just begun." A scripture that has been so very true for me and has such great meaning to me is Proverbs 18:14, which says, "A man's spirit sustains him in sickness, but a crushed spirit who can bear?" So much depends on how we view the circumstances of our lives. If we think I can't do something, then we most likely won't achieve the victory in life that we are looking for. It's so very important to keep your thoughts positive, because if you are not careful, one slip of the tongue can cause a lot of damage. That is also why it's so vitally important to surround yourself with positive thinking people. It's so easy to let the wrong attitude rub off on you and set you on the wrong path.

We all have a designated path that we travel, but sometimes we get sidetracked and step off course. That's when God steps in and gets us heading in the right direction. God knows the end from the beginning, so it's very important that we stay focused and remain on the path that God has placed us on and not let others lure us away from our true calling. Your friends or parents might have a different idea for your life, but in your heart you know just what God is calling you to do for His glory. It's up to you who you follow in your life--your friends or God. In the book of Galatians Paul asked rhetorically, "Am I now trying to win the approval of men or of God?"

God has sure brought me a mighty long way, baby. You might have a testimony of how God has brought you from a mighty long way also. I often think about all the things that I couldn't do for myself but now can, things we take for granted every day of our lives, like making the bed, getting dressed, making my own breakfast. Basically, doing things for myself the way I want them done. That was one of the biggest problems that I encountered before I gained the courage to speak up for myself and not let others take advantage of me just because I am disabled. Some people who don't understand where you are coming from will try to do that if you seem to be an easy target. Fortunately not all people are like that. If you are fortunate to be friends with good people, like I am, give God praise and thanks for bringing them into your life. Proverbs 11:25 tells us that "he who refreshes others will also be refreshed himself." When you have the support of good friends, it makes getting through the difficult times much more bearable. The support of a friend can do so much for one's self-esteem. Just knowing that the other person cares and is there for you means so very much to one's heart.

Chapter 7: Ministry

It is food for the soul to help those who are less fortunate. The help doesn't necessarily have to be money. Even a simple kind word can do a world of good. We should all encourage one another to give of ourselves because I think it is impossible be selfish and happy at the same time. As it says in the Bible in Luke 6:38, "Give and it shall be given to you, a good measure, pressed down, shaken together, and running over will be poured into your lap. For with the measure you use it shall be measured to you." Don't focus your mind so much on earthly things, because you are just passing through this world. The world we dwell in now is not our home; our citizenship is in heaven. In 1 John it says, "Greater is He who is in us than He who is in the world." The devil has some power but Jesus has all power and authority so what ever the devil may throw at you, don't fear; he will never prevail. Jesus reminds us of this in Luke 10:19: "I have given you power to tread over all the power of the enemy."

I am sure we are all familiar with the Golden Rule: "Do onto others as you would have others do unto you." God is not looking for perfection in any one of us. He is simply looking for persistence in all we do. We can't be a powerful testimony for God when there is self-pity in our lives. We cannot act all religious on Sunday and then go back to acting in a carnal, fleshly way Monday through Saturday. God made the statement in James 1:24 describing a man who "after looking at his face in the mirror goes away and immediately forgets what he looks like." That is what we do when we see a problem but don't fix it right away. Sometimes we never fix it, and then it gets all rotten in us, much like an apple or banana that has been left too long.

We cannot be a powerful testimony when we are holding resentment and bitterness in our hearts. God is our power source. If we do not forgive others and do good for others, we become disconnected from the power source. If a lamp is not plugged in it will not give light. In the same way, if we are not plugged in to our power source, we can't produce light either. Like it says in the Bible in Matthew 5:16, "Let your light shine before men that they may see your good deeds and praise your father in heaven." We must stay plugged in to the power source at all times. We should not spend so much time focusing on what God has not yet done for us yet that we forget all that He has done for us. In God's Word He promises He will repay us double for our trouble. Look at Job in the Bible—he lost everything, but God gave him back twice as much as he lost. In the same way, I am much like Job, I have gained so much, but on the other hand I have lost so much also.

God gives us many opportunities to serve others. Notice that I didn't say to serve Him, because He told us in the Bible in the book of Mark that He did not come to be served, but to serve others. With our eyes and ears open we can see and hear the many ways God is demonstrating this every day. The Bible tells us in Matthew 13:19, "When anyone hears the message about the kingdom and does not understand it, the evil one comes and snatches away what was sown in his heart. This is the seed sown along the path."

I am thankful that God has given me another chance in life to do things better and to treat people better. I try to treat others as I would want them to treat me. I might miss the mark occasionally, but I do try to be more mindful of doing and being good to others. James 2:14-26 states, "Faith without works is dead." We must all strive to be a blessing to others and to speak kind words to everyone. The Bible tells us that we just might be entertaining angels without even knowing it. If people treat you badly, that is the time to do good unto them. As Romans 12:21 tells us, "Overcome evil with good."

Colossians 3:23 says, "In whatever you do, work at it with your whole heart, as though working for the Lord, not man." How do you work with your own heart in your life? I do it when I work out to regain what I lost when I was shot. I also give it my very best effort every time that I give my monthly readings in church. Sometimes I choose a poem to read, or it might be a scripture from the Bible, or it might be something that I have written myself. They call my monthly readings "words of encouragement." Isn't it remarkable how God can use someone who is hurting in so many ways to give encouragement to other people who might also be hurting? We also benefit when we work with our whole heart for others. For example, when you or I go to the hospital to encourage someone who is hurting physically, they often end up encouraging us emotionally. I know that even though I am hurting in many ways I still manage to encourage others, and so can you.

I have heard that there is a power that is released from people who are hurting. The power is transferred to the well person from the sick person, which in turn encourages the well person. It's a very strange concept, and it's difficult for me to even begin to understand how it works, but I believe that it is true because I have had people come to me in church and tell me how much that I help them and encourage them. My friend Pastor Barry Garrett once told me what a source of strength I am for him. I can see how when others could be inspired by seeing all that I have over-come and accomplished. God blesses us so that we might bless others. In the Bible it even speaks in 1 Corinthians 1:27 about how God uses the weak things of the world to shame the strong. I have found in my own life over the last 12 years the truth of this state-ment. T.D. Jakes said, "Just because you lost the life that you once had doesn't mean that you have no life before you." Before all of this happened to me I was not sure at all what my purpose in life was, but now I know from a revelation that God gave me that my purpose in life is to be a helper to people who need motivation to overcome any obstacle that they might be facing in life. People in your life might tell you, "No, it can never happen," but if you walk by faith and not by sight, you can do all things.

The Bible tells us in 1 Corinthians 13:4, "Love is patient, love is kind, it does not envy, it does not boast, it is not proud. It is not rude, it is not self-seeking, it is not easily angered, it keeps no re-cord of wrongs. Love does not delight in evil, but rejoices with the truth. It always protects, always trusts, always hopes, always per-severes." Sometimes I wonder, and maybe you do as well, if God really exists. But then I look at all of the beautiful Creation and I know it didn't just get here by itself. The Bible says that we walk by faith and not by sight. So many people today make the mistake of believing in only what the eye can see, but as Christian people we must broaden our horizons. This world that we live in now is not all that there is. There is something beyond this life we are now living, and when we cross over into the next dimension, we will see for ourselves with our very own eyes just what the Bible speaks of.

Before we come to the life beyond this one, we must strive to live our best life here on Earth. There are many ways we fail to do this. for example, have you ever said something you wished you could take back? Many times in my own life I have said something and after I spoke the words I wished with my whole heart that I could take them back. Proverbs 18:21 tells us, "The tongue has the power of death and life, and those who love it will eat its fruit." I like to think that's why God gave us two ears and one mouth--so we listen more than we speak.

Forgiveness, of ourselves and others, plays an enormous role in how we live our lives according to God's wishes for us. When we refuse to forgive, it's like having glue stuck to the bottom of your shoe—it hinders us from going forward in our lives. When you are tempted to be unforgiving or not show mercy, just think to yourself how many times God has forgiven you and how many times God has shown you mercy. We should do the very same thing for each other. In Matthew 25:40, Jesus tells us the King (God) will say, "'Whatever you did for one of the least of these brothers and sisters of mine, you did for me.'" I know from experience what it's like to be wronged, but there comes a time when you and I must learn to move on and let it go.

Joyce Meyer once said, "Deadly emotions just bury the lie. But they never die." That is why it's so vitally important for us to forgive others who have wronged us. No, it is not easy to forgive others when they have done wrong to you. Especially when the thing that they did to hurt you was so traumatic and turned your life upside down and shattered it all into pieces, like a broken glass. It can be so difficult to forgive when your flesh keeps telling you that you just can't because you have been wronged in such a devastating way. But no matter how hard it might be forgive others their trespasses, the Bible tells us in the Lord's Prayer to forgive others just as the Lord has forgiven us. It was VERY hard for me to come to the point in my life where I could truly say to myself with all confidence that I have forgiven the person from my heart who shot me, but if I can find it in my heart to forgive that person— who did me wrong for no reason, except that of the jealousy and bitterness and selfishness that he possessed in his heart—you can also grant forgiveness to those who have wronged you, no matter how hard and no matter how much it hurts to do so. It is the only way to truly get on with your own life.

Forgiveness is one of the hardest things God tells us to grant to one another, because our human instinct is to get that person back for what He or she did. It's also one of Jesus's commands to us in the Bible. Notice He did not say to forgive IF; Jesus put a period after the word forgive. That means it's the end of the discussion. I think of Matthew 18:21, where Peter asks the Lord, "How many times should I forgive my brother when he sins against me? Up to seven times?" Jesus replied to Peter's questions by saying, "I tell you, not seven times, but seventy times seven."

Psalm 45:1 says, "My tongue is the pen of a ready writer." In the same exact way my hands are the pen of a ready writer. I know that this might sound a little bit strange, but God gives me the ideas and words, so my hands are those of a ready writer. What I have done in this book is given you some phrases and metaphors to compare to the real thing--your life.

Perhaps you've heard the expression, "It is the man that makes the heart." I think it should be turned around and said like this: "It is the heart that makes the man." What that means to me is that what is in a man's heart will eventually come out. If a person's heart is filled with goodness and gratefulness, that is what will eventually come out. But if the heart is filled with resentment or thoughts of revenge, that too will show itself sooner or later. Joyce Meyer once said, "Where the mind goes the man follows."

In our walk of faith there is a purification process that we must all go through. Before God can use us to bring Him glory, we must first be cleansed of all unrighteousness. That means that, among other things, we must not hold onto bitterness or any type of a grudge against anyone. I am aware that this is easy to say and very hard to do. God knows that it's not an easy thing for us, but He never asks us to do anything that is not in our best interest. He is always closer to us then we think. Just because we can't always feel His presence in our lives doesn't mean that He has left us. He made a promise to us in His Word that He would never leave us, and God is not a man that He would ever lie.

When singers do warm up exercises for their voices, they sometimes warm up by singing the word me, me, me. That is okay for singers to do, but it is very dangerous for you and me to be thinking only of ourselves. Jesus said in the book of Mark (10:45), "I have come to serve and not to be served." That's the attitude we should possess, that of a servant. We need to look upon the interests and needs of others as well as our own, just as the Bible tells us to do in Philippians 2:3: "Do nothing out of selfish ambition or vain conceit, but in humility consider others better than yourself. Each of you should look not only to your own interests, but also to the interests of others." Or you might prefer to think of it this way: "Know yourself. Honor others. Live for Christ."

The time that we spend with God on Sundays should not be viewed as a social gathering with friends, but as a personal time for you and God. Yes, it's a special time during the week when we come into God's presence and leave the cares of the world behind, but it's even more of a personal and special time when we are in God's house to worship and adore him. I don't believe that our Sunday church time with God should be treated as a run-of-the-mill everyday ritual either. Jesus told us to keep the Sabbath day holy. (You might be thinking that traditionally the Sabbath day is Saturday, not Sunday. I would think it's whatever day you devote to your public worship though. So be it Saturday or Sunday that you choose to worship on, I think it should be kept holy, and not treated as a ordinary event in your life.)

A powerful part of the wonderful hymn "Amazing Grace" is the verse in which it says "I once was lost, but now I am found." I was lost both emotionally and spiritually, but now that I am reborn of the Spirit and not just born of the flesh, I am a whole different person. I am much more considerate of others' feelings and emotions. When I see another person suffering, I try to put myself in their place. That is something that might help you also with your thoughts, because the Bible tells us in Proverbs 23:7, "As a man thinks in his heart, so is he." So to help with selfish way of thinking that our mind tries to deceive us with, try saying to yourself, "That could be me, but thanks be to God, it's not." Or imagine to yourself that you are weaving a threefold tapestry. The first stand of your tapestry will be the love strand, the second strand of your tapestry will be the faith strand, and the third strand will be the most helpful stand of all--the strand of the Word of God. We need the Word of God to direct our path each and every day, not just when we're facing big decisions, but for the small ones as well.

As the Bible tells us in Proverbs 3:5-6, "Trust in the Lord with all your heart, and lean not on your own understanding. In all your ways acknowledge Him, and He shall direct thy path." Faith would also fit into that woven tapestry. In Hebrews 11:6 it says that "Without faith it is impossible to please God, because anyone who comes must believe that He exists and that He rewards those who earnestly seek Him." Are you earnestly seeking God? When you put this threefold tapestry together of love, faith, and the Word of God, it's not easily broken by anything that might cross your path. I truly believe that these three strands do work if they are applied properly in your life, but you cannot just say, "I have faith," because the Bible tells us in James 2:26, "For as the body without the spirit is dead, so faith without works is dead." So it's also very important to do good, as well as to have faith.

In the movie "Fireproof" a character says: "Women are like roses. Treat them right and they will bloom." I guess that could also be said about men. Any person who is treated right will eventually bloom into a beautiful flower. So treat everyone with the respect that you would want to receive in return. Don't be disrespectful to others. Don't be selfish and put your own priorities in life over others'. Always put God first in your life, above all else, like the Bible tells us in Matthew 6:33: "But seek ye first the kingdom of God and his righteousness, and all of these things will be given to you." In John 6:63, Jesus tells us, "The words I speak to you are spirit and life." We should give ear and take heart to everything God tells us to do. The words He tells us are not for His benefit, but our own. When He tells us to forgive others for their wrongdoing, it's not for His benefit that we forgive others, but our own. He tells us in the Book of Mark 11:25 that if we don't forgive others neither will our Heavenly Father forgive us. God knows what's best for us, even if what he asks us to do may be difficult.

What we are is our gift from God. What we become is our gift back to God. I never imagined I would be writing a book to encourage others, or be sharing my life's events with others to encourage and lift their spirits. I'm doing it to help others who are going through their own types of challenges, big and small, and to let you know that if I can go through the fire and the testing of life, you can too. You might not want to, but in Proverbs 16:9 the Bible says, "In his heart a man plans his course, but the Lord determines his steps." When everything that you are facing in life seems impossible, just remember this: You can always call on the name of our Lord and Savior for His help and strength.

If you sweep dirt under the living room rug, it's still there even if you can no longer see it, right? Well, it's the same way when we don't forgive others who have done us wrong. Though we may think we have swept it under the rug, the resentment is still there within us. It may be hidden for now, but it will eventually come out. My pastor says, what's on the inside of us will eventually come out, no matter how we try and hide it and act like everything is okay. Having an unforgiving spirit is much like swallowing poison--it tastes bad and will eventually kill you.

Another idea that God gave me was the "open hand" concept. When you or I find something or someone in life that we want or think we need, our tendency it to want to hold tightly onto it. But when we hold tightly onto things, we tend to lose them. For example, when a dog jumps up on you and you grab his paws, he squirms and tries to get away. Instead, if you offer an open hand, the dog will feel safe in your presence. In the same way, we can put the open hand theory into practice in our lives. I know from personal experience that this is very hard to do. I think the song written by Sting sums it up when it says so plainly to us, "If you love someone, set them free." If they come back to you it was meant to be, and if not then it wasn't.

Maybe you are like me and feel the same way about the gospel of God (I learned from my pastor that "gospel" means "good news."). The scripture I am referring to is out of the book of Jeremiah 20: 9-10: "His word is like fire shut up in my bones." I have an insatiable urge to preach the gospel. To those of you who have never experienced that feeling, it's unexplainable. It's a feeling that one experiences way down deep in their spirit. Only the one who has ever experienced it can explain it. It's like no other feeling that I've ever had. You have to feel it to believe it! God is the same way—you have to experience His power for yourself. You can't get the same effect if someone tells you about the goodness of God. You must experience it for yourself. It's just like if a friend shares something great that has happened to them. You may be happy for them, but until it happens to you in your life you will never fully understand the happiness that they have.

A pastor friend of mine said in one of his sermons that God puts dreams and visions in our hearts and when we get a little bit closer to that dream coming to fruition, God moves it back a little bit so that we have something to reach for and work toward. I can identify with that because although I want to do God's will in my life, I have not figured out what that is yet. I am remembering what Victoria Osteen said on television once. She asked a very good question: "How big is your want?" On a scale from one to ten, my want is about an eight or nine, but given time I am quite certain that will grow into a ten. God has given me so very much; I just want to repay Him somehow and tell Him how very thankful that I am for every blessing that He has bestowed unto me. Have you ever experienced this longing deep down inside of your soul, and there was no possible way for you to satisfy it? That's exactly how I feel about all God has given to me in my life.

That brings to mind a song that we sometimes sing in our church. The name of it is "What He's Done for Me." That song really has deep meaning for me, because I know that if it wasn't for the grace of God, I wouldn't be where I am today. To God be all the glory. Thank you for everything, Father God!

Sometimes I think of Jesus as an air traffic controller. In all circumstances in our life we need to stay in constant contact with the air traffic controller. Jesus will lead us and guide us through any storm that might arise in our life. God doesn't always promise us that there will never be turbulance, but he does promise us there will be a smooth landing. It has been said that love fades after a while, even when we get married, but it's just the exact opposite with my relationship to the Lord. There might be some people who can't quit understand where I am coming from, and that's okay. True worship and devotion to God is something that comes with practice, every minute and every day of our life.

Picture in your mind a ladder. We climb each rung one by one, step by step. Our walk with the Lord is like that. We take each step one by one. There may be times in our faith walk that we want to skip a couple of steps in between and climb to a higher level, but unfortunately we are not ready yet. We must each progress at our own rate. I have found this to be true in my own personal walk with the Lord. When I first begin giving readings at my church, I started out by reading a poem that was written by someone else. Now I do my own writing for church readings. Everyone must start somewhere. Even if it's just a small part, give it all you have because God sees your time and your effort. Even the little things matter.

As children we all did connect-the-dots, drawing lines from number to number to create a finished picture. Have you connected the dots in your own personal life? God gives us signs, puts the numbers in place for us. We just need to connect them. We can choose to follow the dots, or we can choose to do what the flesh would desire and ignore God's directions. God always reveals things to us that we are unaware of. God has shown me some things in my own personal life that I would never fathom. God has showed me that in His time frame that I will be preaching His most holy Word more than I am now at my church. So I will do what the farmer does and plant my crop and wait patiently for my harvest to come up, and not to just sit around and do nothing, but actively prepare myself spiritually for what is to come in my very near future.

Chapter 8: God's Provision

Sometimes my life is much like the title of the song by Rev. F. C. Barnes: "Rough Side of the Mountain." I am climbing up the rough side of the mountain. Like the song says, it does get difficult sometimes, so I must hold on to God's powerful hand, because with His help I know I can accomplish anything, and so can you. People who don't have God's power working in their life may wonder where this strength comes from. Paul says in 2 Corinthians 12:9, "But He said to me, 'My grace is sufficient for you, for My power is made perfect in weakness.' Therefore I will boast all the more gladly about my weakness, so that Christ's power may rest on me. That is why for Christ's sake I delight in weakness, in insults, in hardships, in persecutions, in difficulties. For when I am weak, then I am strong."

A song that has significant meaning for me is "Hold On to God's Unchanging Hand." I really like it because it is a confirmation that God always walks with us, regardless of what we are going through in life. He is always with us, directing our path just like the scripture says in Proverbs 3:5, "Trust in the Lord with all your heart, and lean not to your own understanding. In all thy ways acknowledge Him, and He shall direct thy path." I trust in the Lord to direct my path, and He has made my crooked places straight. First I had to make the important decision to follow Him with my whole heart, not half way as some do, with one foot in the church and the other foot in the world. (That's an idea I borrowed from the pastor of a church I once attended.)

Don't set your mind on gossip; rather, set your mind on the gospel of God. We think way too much about the desires of the outer person, when we should be thinking about our inner person. We all make sure every day that the outer person looks good, but how much attention do we give to our inner person? The outer person will eventually die, but our inner person lives forever. Preparation time is never wasted time. If we desire something, we need to prepare for it. If we go to a job interview, we prepare for the questions we think we might be asked. If we are running in a marathon, we prepare for that by exercising and eating healthy. In the same way, we need to get ourselves prepared for eternity. We get so caught up in the things of this world that we forget the most important one of all--where we will spend our eternal life. As it says in the Bible in Ecclesiastes:

"There is a time for every activity under heaven.
A time to be born and a time to die,
A time to plant and a time to uproot,
A time to kill and a time to heal,
A time to tear down and a time to build,
A time to weep and a time to laugh,
A time to mourn and a time to dance,
A time to scatter stones and a time to gather them,
A time to embrace and a time to refrain,
A time to search and a time to give up,
A time to keep and a time to throw away,
A time to tear and a time to mend,

A time to be silent and a time to speak,
A time to love and a time to hate,
A time for war and a time for peace."

The verse "a time to kill and a time to heal" has a very significant meaning for me because I infer from it that there is a certain time when God will totally heal my whole body from everything that's holding me back from where I am supposed to be. Have you ever had that feeling that where you are right now in life is not where God wants you? I am not speaking only in a physical sense, but in an emotional sense as well. God put in my heart that I am going to be doing more for Him in due time, but (yes, that's the word I get frustrated with, the word "but") it has to be in the time He has appointed, not in man's time frame but His time frame, because God's timing is perfect in everything. God knows what is best for us in every situation. I am sure that I am just not speaking for myself when I say life can be a jigsaw puzzle at times for all of us figuring out what God's will is for our lives, but I have found that if I just give God all of the pieces, He will figure out where they all fit perfectly. I guess you could also compare life to a Rubik's cube—we can twist and turn it all day, but if we do not know how it goes we won't be successful. So we must try not to worry so much about things we don't have any control over. We must just do as the Bible tells us to do in 1 Peter 5:7: "Cast all of your cares upon him, because He careth for you." As it says in the Bible in Psalm 30:5, "Weeping may endure for a night, but joy cometh in the morning."

Another promise God gives to us in Lamentations 3:25 tells us that the Lord is good to those whose hope is in Him, to those who seek Him. I seek his guidance and wisdom for the course of my life every day. I don't make my decisions all by myself, but instead I try to involve God in every decision of my life, from the smallest decision to the biggest. It's not common now for people to ask themselves, "What would Jesus do in this situation?" The scriptures tell us in Proverbs 8:17, "I love those who love me, and those who seek me find me." I start out my mornings spending time with God in prayer and reading His Word to us, and I can't even begin to tell you how very much it helps me throughout the day when I first prepare for the day that lies ahead of me.

We are sure to sin against God at least once in a day if not more. (I am just using the number one as an example; you can fill in the number for yourself however you see fit.) The Bible even tells us in Proverbs 28:13 that "he that covereth his sins shall not prosper." We might get away with what we have done or said wrong for a while, and think to ourselves that we have put one over on God, but how many of you know that you can never fool God? We all have heard the saying, "You can fool some of the people some of the time, but you can't fool all of the people all of the time." In the same exact way, we cannot fool God, but rather should revere Him. He knows and sees everything we do and fail to do. We can't get away with anything.

As it says in the book of Romans 12:21, "Be not overcome of evil, but overcome evil with good." God doesn't promise to stop every storm that comes into our lives, but He does promise to be with us in every step we take. I would suggest to you all to live every day on earth as if it was your last day, because it very well might be. I had no idea on June 11 what I was about to go through, but thanks be to God I didn't have to go through it all alone. To remind you of all the great and wonderful works our Lord has done for you in your life, you may want to try keeping a journal of all his good works. Then you can reflect on it when times get hard, as they so often do.

Hebrews 13: 5 reminds us, "I will never leave you or forsake you." That verse is so comforting to me, because it reminds me that God is always with me no matter the circumstance, and that He is always with us even when we don't feel His presence. You don't always have to feel His presence to know that He is always there with you in your daily activities. Love is not always a warm fuzzy feeling that we get. In fact, love is not just a feeling we sometimes get, but rather it's a willing heart that tells God, "I might not like the situation that I am in, but I trust You completely in spite of the situation. I will praise and give thanks to You regardless of my circumstance." Always remember that God is always with us and he sees exactly what we are going through.

Another Bible verse that really ministers to my soul is Romans 8:37. It tells us that we are "more than conquerors" through Him who loved us first. That tells me that no matter what we are going through in life, good or bad, God is always with us. Ecclesiastes 7:14 says, "When times are good be happy, but when times are bad, consider God has made the one as well as the other." Additionally, 1 Thessalonians 5:16 tells us to "Be joyful always, pray continually, give thanks in all circumstances, for this is God's will for you in Christ Jesus." I know that God doesn't ask for the bad things that happen in my life, but he will be with me in those times.

It can sometimes be difficult for me to give thanks to God for the situation I am currently in, having to re-familiarize myself with doing everything I once knew so well, but as the saying goes, "Everything happens for a reason." I have heard it said by Pastor Joel Osteen, "Things don't happen to us, they happen for us." He also gives this very wise piece of advice: "Never start out your day in a neutral mindset, because you become what you believe." The Bible tells us our thoughts determine our future, so if we think negatively, then negative things will come to pass in our lives. Proverbs 23:7 declares, "As a man thinks in his heart, so is he." For more on the thoughts and the mind, I suggest that you read Battlefield of the Mind by Joyce Meyer.

I heard once that the word F. E. A. R. stands for False Emotions Appearing Real. That's true for all of us at one time or another. I struggle from time to time with the fear of the unknown.

When we worry, it tells God that we don't trust Him to supply all of our needs. God promises that He will be true to His word in Numbers 23:19, saying, "God is not a man that He should lie." The Bible also says, in Philippians 4:19, "But my God shall supply all your needs according to His riches and glory in Christ Jesus."

When we experience fear, we have a tendency to focus our attention on how big our problems are, when we should be focused instead on how big our God is and how much He can do. This is the mistake I make sometimes, and I would venture to say that you are probably guilty of it as well. I also have a tendency to focus way too much on what God can do for me and give me, to the extent that I lose focus on just being His child. In other words, I sometimes get too wrapped up in what I can get from God, rather than just seeking Him for who He is in my life. Please don't misunderstand me, material things are nice, but material attainment should not be our main reason for seeking God's face.

I have a friend at my church who had to relearn how to walk just as I have. He was first in a wheelchair for a while and now he has graduated to using a walker. I was thinking about how God takes us through our circumstances in stages. If you think back to when you were an infant and just learning how to walk and talk and do things on your own, you realize we did not achieve this all at once. We all had to go through that process of learning how. Just as when we learn anything new, there are directions that we must follow in life.

Here's another way of looking at it. When you or I purchase an item that requires assembly, we receive a book of directions and steps to read and follow. When we reach the end of our project we know that we have followed the directions correctly if all the parts fit together and work properly. In the same way, we know that we have followed God's direction if everything fits together properly. The Bible tells us in Proverbs 1:7, "The fear of the Lord is the beginning of knowledge, but fools despise wisdom and instruction."

Whatever instruction we receive from the Lord, we should always follow it. God will never prompt us to do something that we are incapable of doing, and of course He will always be with us helping us and leading us and guiding us. In His most holy Word He told us in Hebrews 13:4, "Never will I leave thee or forsake thee." Those reassuring words let me know that in my own personal life God will not only see me through the storm, but He will also walk with me on my way through it to my next destination. God does not promise to stop every storm that occurs in our lives, but He does promise to always walk with us and help us to see our way through it clearly.

Give this question some very serious thought: What two words in the English language would you consider to be the most powerful or the most confidence-building for you? After giving this much thought I came up with the words BUT GOD! They remind me that no matter what I'm facing in life, God is always with me. I have heard it said that He goes before us, making sure that our steps are straight and that we will not stumble and fall.

Many selections from the Bible help to give me confidence. For example, I really appreciate this verse from Psalm 1, which says, "Blessed is the man who walketh not in the counsel of the wicked nor standeth in the way of sinners, but his delight is in the law of the Lord, and on that law he meditates day and night. For he shall be like a tree planted by the rivers of water to bringeth forth fruit in his own season, whose leaf shall not wither and what so ever he doeth shall prosper." That tells me that if what I am doing pleases God in my daily life, I shall prosper and reap the benefits from doing so. The Bible tells us in Proverbs 28:13 that "he who conceals his sins does not prosper, but whoever confesses and renounces them finds mercy." God appreciates our honesty so be truthful to Him about all things, even your trespasses.

I heard this very encouraging statement from Joel Osteen: "God is not looking at how we messed things up; He is looking at how to clean them up." Like everyone, I sometimes really make a big mess of things. For example, I have treated the people that were the closest to me badly at times. If I could, I would take back every wrong thing that I've ever done to others. If only it were that easy! What I can do is tell them all how sorry that I am for my wrong behavior, and of course also tell God how sorry I am. That brings to my mind 1st John 1:9, "If we confess our sins, He is faithful and just and will forgive us our sins and purify us from all unrighteousness." I am so sorry for my selfish behavior, please forgive me my Father God and my family.

1 Corinthians 1:25 says, "For the foolishness of God is wiser then man's wisdom and the weakness of God is stronger than man's strength." I am a witness to that in my own life, because I know that the strength that I have is not that of my own, but rather it is God's strength that carries me through every day. I know it is only God's grace and mercy that enable me to do what I do every day and not give up. If you think this way He will also give you the ability to do the impossible.

Another of my favorite Joel Osteen statements is: "If you can see the invisible, God can do the impossible." That's so true. This book you are reading was written by someone who could see the invisible, and God did the impossible in my life. Just a few years ago, nobody dreamed that I would be where I am today, not even me. I never believed I'd be doing so well. I give all the credit to God, and He deserves every bit of it.

My feelings for Jesus are expressed in Whitney Houston's song, "I Will Always Love You." He has done so very much for me. I just wish that I could personally thank Him for it all. Oh yes, I know that I can thank Him in my prayers, which I do, but I just wish I could thank Him face-to-face for all His many wonderful benefits that He has rendered to me. Most everyone, doctors included, said that there was no possible way I would recover from my injury and be normal again, but now I know that God is the

God of the "I can's." Yes, everyone was correct when they sad that I couldn't recover on my own. However, I did not go through this alone at al—Jesus has been with me every step of the way, just like in the poem "Footprint." In the poem, as person asks Jesus why, in the most difficult times in his life, He only saw one set of footprints in the sand? Jesus replied, "When you saw only one set of footprints in the sand, it was then that I carried you." In the same exact way, Jesus has carried me through so many difficult times in my life. I guess that you might say I have a GPS—no, not global positioning system, but God's protection system. I have gone through so many things I know I could have never survived on my own.

One thing that we take for granted every day is the ability God has given us to remember things from our past, including what we did just the previous day. I would give anything to have that given back to me. I do remember a lot of things from my past, but there are many, many important events that have been erased from my memory. And of course there are some things I would like to forget, just as you would. We don't always know how blessed we are by something until that thing is gone. I have heard people say if I only had a lot of money then I would be happy. But money alone doesn't guarantee happiness. No amount of money can buy good health. So if you have your health and your memory, know that you are a blessed beyond belief. I would give anything to have that once again, so never take it for granted. I did, and now I can relate to Cher's song, "If I could turn back time." I so wish I could have those days given back to me. Don't be like me and have to wish for them to be given back to you.

A good friend of mine made a very interesting comment in one of his sermons. He said that God can reach back into your life and bring forth things that were stolen from you by the devil. I have found that to be true in my own life, because God has given me back so very much that I lost on the day that I was hurt. I heard it said once that whatever the devil stole from us, he must repay it to us sevenfold.

Why am I in the same exact situation that I was before at some other time in my life? I don't think that I am the only person to ever wonder this. Why does God put us in the same exact situation that we found our self in years ago? I think He does this so that we can redo things in a better way than we did before. The picture that God put in my mind was that of a clock with the hands on it turning counterclockwise. God has that ability to turn back the hands of time for us. It's important to live for the present day, yes, but it also important to be mindful of the future. Don't focus your energy on things that will not matter much in the long run; remember to consider your future. Everyone, me included, likes to live for today, but if I would have known then what I know now, I would have done things so differently.

James 4:14-17 comes to mind: "Why you do not even know what will happen tomorrow. What is your life? You are a mist that appears for a little while and then vanishes." Instead you ought to say, 'If it is the Lord's will, I will live and do this or that." We are not our own; we have been bought with a price that no one could ever pay. There was only one perfect individual, and He was the atoning sacrifice for all of our sins. He died on the cross over two thousand years ago for us. When Jesus was in the garden of Gethsemane the Bible says that He sweated great drops of blood. Those great drops of blood were from the heaviness He felt from all of our sins that He took upon himself.

Our minds are kind of like lawn mowers (I admit that sounds strange, but bear with me). When you or I are going to mow our lawns our lawn mower needs fuel in it to operate properly, correct? Well, in the very same way, we also need spiritual fuel to keep moving forward. If we don't take the time each day to refuel on God's word, we will eventually run out of spiritual gas and no longer have the desire to press on through adversity. It's very important that we take the time in the morning when we rise out of bed to refuel our minds on God's word, because it's very easy for us to get carried away by a worldly mentality of how we should operate.

Not everyone takes the time to refuel on God's word every day, but we all have to make a choice about how we spend our time and energy. Not everyone will have the same priorities as you. Some people live their life day by day, while others live their life for some future dream. So, as Paul says in Romans 14:5, "One man considers one day more sacred than another, another man considers every day alike. Each one should be fully convinced in his own mind."

If you are going through something troubling in life, do like the old gospel song says and take it "one day at a time" with "sweet Jesus." God will be with you in every situation to overcome every adversity that the devil has put on you. We must stay connected to God in every way in our life. He is the gas tank that keeps the lawn mower running and if the gas runs out, there we are stranded with no one to call on. So keep your tank filled with the Word of God. God will never lead us in the wrong direction; we just have to trust in Him. As the Bible tells us in Proverbs 3:5-6, "Trust in the Lord with all thine heart, and lean not on thine own understanding. In all thy ways acknowledge Him, and He will direct thy path." God will direct our steps. We just need to let him.

You and I make choices in our lives each and every moment from the time that we get up in the morning until we go to bed at night, but the most important choice that we will ever make is accepting Jesus as our Lord and personal Savior. We might think we can run our own life, but in the end we may make a mess of things and then God has to clean up after us. In my own life God cleaned up the big mess that I made of everything. I am so glad that God didn't say these words to me: "Oh well, too bad my child; that's the way it goes." Instead, thank God for His mercy, which endures forever.

Psalm 116 articulates what I feel in my heart so strongly: "What shall I return to the Lord for all of his goodness to me?" This book is written in God's honor. I accept whatever His will is for my future.

Chapter 9: Thankfulness

Proverbs 16:9 says, "In his heart a man plans his course, but the Lord determines his steps." That verse speaks to my heart in so many ways because it so plainly states that although we may have our own plans for the future, in the grand scheme of things God's plan for our lives will always take precedence. It's kind of a vulnerable and uneasy position for anybody to be in, to know that you are not really in control of your own life as much as you thought you were. I say with all gladness of heart that I am so very thankful and grateful that just as the star shone on Mary when she was giving birth to Jesus, Jesus has shone upon me for the last 15 years while I have been climbing this extremely steep mountain to recovery. Despite all of the difficulties I encounter every day, I still try to keep a positive attitude because, after all, I could have died that day in June 1999. Yes, I know that I have lost a lot in my life, but thanks be to God that I still have my life. I have had some bad days, but the good days far outweigh them, so I say, "Thank You, Lord. Thank You, Lord, for watching over me and hiding me in Your pavilion." (Psalm 27:5 says, "For in the time of trouble He shall hide me in his pavilion.")

We should always have a thankful attitude. In 1 Thessalonians 4:18 the Bible tells us that "in every circumstance" we are to give thanks—not in some circumstances, not in certain circumstances when we feel like giving thanks, but in ALL circumstances that we encounter in life. You may wonder how I can be thankful after the death of my fiancé. When I was a little girl, I loved the story of Cinderella. I loved it so much that David and I were going to have a Cinderella-themed wedding. He was my real-life Prince Charming, and we were going to live happily ever after. As hard as it was for me to lose him, I give all the thanks to God that I met him. Many people never have the opportunity to know someone as wonderful as he was. Even though the time that we had together was short, I am just so very thankful for the time I had with David. When I think of him I am reminded of the Stephanie Mills song, "I Never Knew Love Like this Before."

I often meditate on the subject of gratitude. Thinking of the saying, "thanks-giving is thanks-living" inspires me to ask myself if I have a thankful attitude and a thankful spirit. "Life is God's gift to us; what we choose to do with that life is our gift to God," Father Frederic Pisegna said on his TV show, "Live with Passion." Joel Osteen talks about how it's so important that we have the right perspective on our life. For instance, if we can walk by ourselves we should give thanks to God for that. If we can go to the kitchen and prepare a meal for ourselves and then sit down and eat it and taste what we have made to eat, we should give thanks to God for that. Take it from someone who knows just what they are missing. There are so many mundane, everyday things that seem so average and repetitious to us, but as the wise saying goes, we need to stop and smell the roses. Life might not always be fair, but God is just and fair, for He never changes. Hebrews 13:8 tells us that Jesus is "the same yesterday, today, and forever." People, on the other hand, might tell you one thing one day and then do something totally different the next day, but I guess that is just part of the flawed human nature that dwells within us.

One night while lying in bed I was thinking about when Jesus raised Lazarus from the dead. I can relate to that story because I've was almost dead myself--or so the doctors thought anyway! When Jesus talked to Mary and Martha, He asked them the question, "DO YOU BELIEVE?" Their response was, "Yes, Lord, we believe that we will see the glory of God." In the very same way, I have seen the glory of God revealed in the healing that has taken place so far in my body. I believe that God's not through yet by any means in my life and my healing. In Isaiah 38:16 it says: "You restored me to health and let me live." I lived so that I would be a testimony to others about God's goodness and what he can do.

There are many ways to practice gratitude for the gifts God has given you. When we show gratitude to others, we are not only saying "thank you" to the person who did us a favor, but we are also honoring God. Yes, it's very hard to be grateful during the not-so-good times in life, but it's those hard times that stretch our faith and make us who we are. If everything in life were easy, our faith would not grow. It's when we are tested during the unpleasant times in our lives and our faith is tried that we grow.

Just now as I sit at my desk typing this, I was trying to think of a Bible verse that would tie into with what I want to say next, and I came across a greeting card that I forgot to send for Thanksgiving. On the card is this Bible verse: "Give thanks to the Lord for His unfailing love and His wonderful deeds." We must keep everything fresh in our life, or it will eventually get old. Take, for example, the condo that my mom and dad purchased two years ago. I could have forgotten God's blessing of how our realtor found this lovely home for us, but I kept it fresh in my memory, remembering where we lived before and just how very grateful and thankful I am to live here. So remember where you were at one time in your life, and take time to thank God for where you are right now. That is one of the many things that I have learned and experienced in my walk with the Lord. It does not come to my brain automatically, though; I have to keep the thought fresh in my mind or my lovely home will become old and routine. In the the book of James it tells us that "every good and every perfect gift comes from above."

The blessings that God has bestowed unto me are not all material blessings. The most valuable gift is my faith and just how much I have grown spiritually. My friend Kim and I were talking about how much that I have grown spiritually since she started working with me back in 2003. She mentioned how fortunate I am to have much of my memory intact. She once worked with a couple who had Alzheimer's disease, so she saw just what an awful thing it is when your mind does not work the way it is supposed to. I do forget some things, but for the most part my memory is pretty good, given the circumstances and all that I have been through, and seeing as most of the doctors thought that I was a goner. Of course I know know that man does not determine your future--God determines it. The Bible tells us, in Jeremiah 1:5, "Before I formed you in the belly, I knew thee, and before thou camest forth out of the womb, I sanctified thee, and I ordained thee a prophet unto the nations."

It's about a week before Christmas now, and everyone is so focused on their Christmas gifts, but that's not what Christmas is about—or at least it shouldn't be. It should be about all the blessings that God has bestowed on us in the past year. I used to be so focused on the gifts that I forgot the reason for the Christmas season. Remember at this time of year and all times to count all of your blessings. You might not have everything in life that you want, but be thankful for what you do have, because many would be glad to trade places with you. That is something I must work on as well, because I think too much about what I have lost, and I forget to appreciate and be thankful for all that I do have in life. So many people would be glad to trade places with me. Instead of grumbling and being sour, we must learn to work through the hard times and press on toward the mark. As Paul tells us in Philippians 3:13-14, "Brethren I count not myself to have apprehended it, but this one thing I do: forgetting those things which are behind, and reaching forth unto those things which are before, I press toward the mark for the prize of the high calling of God in Christ Jesus." What does giving up accomplish in the long run? God sees what we will become, not just us as we are now, and that should be encouraging in and of itself.

I compare my life's events to a glass that shatters and is broken into pieces. When something drops and is broken, it all happens in a split second, and there is a big mess left to clean up. There has also been a big mess left for me to clean up from the day I was shot. I know that some of my friends and family members think that I am always too serious in life and should have more fun. The truth is I have fun in life every day; I am just so just grateful to be given this chance. I just don't find it fun to be unproductive. Coming as close to death as I did has an effect on you that is unexplainable to one who has never experienced it.

Many people probably wonder how I can be at peace, given my situation. I just always remember that I have the help of the Holy Spirit, who intercedes for me in everything I do. I also think of this principle: I am way too blessed in life to be stressed. Yes, there is no doubt about it, things in my life are hard, but they could be a lot harder. I encourage you to try looking at your own life that way, if you have to overcome adversities like I do.

One recent Sunday morning this appeared in my church's bulletin: "Happy moments—praise God. Difficult moments—seek God. Quiet moments—worship God. Painful moments—trust God. Every moment—thank God." It's easy to be appreciative of everything He gives to us for a little while, but if we're not careful we can let a self-centered attitude take root in our hearts. We should always be grateful and thankful for everything God has blessed us with, because with the twinkling of an eye God can remove all His blessing that He has given us. Just as easily as He can give them to His children, He can also remove them from our grasp.

Once you have, with God's help, acquired many blessings, don't think that you can stop thanking and praising God for everything He has given you. That's not how it works; the praise it took you to get where you are is also the praise that is required to keep you there. If you are grateful for all that God has done for you, then you probably wish, like me, that there was some way that you could thank Him in this physical realm that we live in. Unfortunately, the only sacrifice here on earth that we can offer to Him is our precious time. That is why it is so important, every day, to spend quality time with God. God is not looking for quantity time from us; what He wants is quality time. When we start the day praising God and give Him the time He so deserves, the whole day ends up being more productive.

I have heard it said, "Get your praise on, because when praises go up to God, blessings will come down." It's easy for us to praise God when we are standing on the mountain top, but it's not so easy to praise God when we are in the valley. When our feelings tell us we don't have anything to praise God for, that is the time more than ever to pray and tell God how very thankful you are for everything He has helped you with and healed your body from. One of the many blessings that come from God is physical healing to your body. I am a witness to that, because I was never supposed to talk or walk or eat or even be able to tell you the goodness of God and all He has done for me in my life. When the doctors basically gave up on me, after they had done all that they could do, that's when God stepped in and took hold of the steering wheel; He took over from that point.

Remember that song form the 80s by the group Cinderella, "Don't Know What You Got Until It's Gone"? That could be the soundtrack to my life! I had no idea of what I had until it was taken from me, and now that I have lost so much, I see and appreciate all that I did have even more. In many cases you have to hit the very bottom of the barrel of life, so to speak, before you can ever be totally grateful for all that God has so graciously blessed you with. If you have a job, be grateful for that. I have heard people complain about their jobs, but so many people would be grateful for any job at all. Joel Olsteen once said, "When we complain, we shall remain, but when we praise, we will be raised." There are those who would love to lead a normal life and get up every morning and go to a job, but due to health complications or unemployment they can't. So if you are one of the fortunate people that can, be glad and rejoice and thank the Lord for His goodness that He has blessed you with.

Sometimes when I am experiencing the work of God in my life, I find myself preparing for the other shoe to eventually fall. There is nothing wrong with being prepared, but don't take preparations to the extreme. Don't always think that things are too good to be true. Maybe God is placing you in a different place in your life, because He feels that you suffered and went through enough bad times, and now it's time for good to come into your life. Right now, in my own life, I am experiencing really great and unbelievable things. But I also find myself thinking "What if?" so much that I sometimes don't enjoy the blessings. What if this doesn't work out? What if I didn't do the right thing or say the proper words? This kind of thinking is just one of the many tricks that the devil uses to steal our happiness from us. We get so caught up in the "what if"s that we don't enjoy the moment that God has given to us.

Sometimes things happen to us that we can't understand. In this situation Deuteronomy 29:29 tells us, "The secret things belong to the Lord." I have been in situations that I just can't even begin to understand. Why, when my life was finally starting to turn around for the better, did I get hit so hard with all these adversities? Why do I have to go through all this? 1 Thessalonians says, "In everything give thanks!" It would have been so very easy to become bitter toward God for allowing those horrible situations to come across my path in life. Just when I thought I was getting it all together I had all these unfortunate things happen to me. I lost my fiancé. I lost my ability to walk and have good balance. I lost my sense of smell. I lost my hearing ability in my left ear. But like Job said in the Bible, "The Lord gave, and the Lord hath taken away." So I would say to everyone, rejoice and give thanks, even when you don't want to. Be thankful when the Lord gives to you, but also give thanks in the circumstances that have come upon your life that you didn't ask for. When we show love and kindness to one another it makes getting through the rough and tough times in life so much easier.

Life can seem like a see-saw with all its ups and downs, but if there were only good and happy times in our lives we would not really appreciate all of God's blessings. We would be so accustomed to all His great and many blessings that we would take them for granted. Take care to not take even the littlest blessing in your life for granted. Appreciate your ability to smell all of the beautiful flowers, or go into a store and smell the perfume and aroma of food cooking in the kitchen. It's possible for tragedy to strike at any time, so don't take those you love for granted. James 4:14 says, "whereas ye know not what shall be on the morrow for what is your life? It is even a vapor that appearth for a little time and then vanisheth away." Tell people you love them today, because we never know what tomorrow will bring. I just wish that I didn't have to find that out the hard way, but then again some things must be learned by experience. Isaiah 48:10 says, "See, I have refined you, though not as silver. I have tested you in the furnace of affliction."

One night as I was lying in bed, I thought to myself about the reasons why we don't always get what we want in life. The first reason I remember reading in the Bible was that it's not God's timing yet. The second reason is that it's not His will for your life. I never understood that until just recently. His will in your life might be as simple as choosing a line of work, or it might be more of a complicated situation like choosing a spouse. In whatever decisions you are trying to make, be sure to involve God's opinion, because He knows what is best for us better than we do. You might think that you know what's best for you but I ask you: Who created you? In Jeremiah 1:5 it says, "Before I formed you in the womb I knew you, before you were born I set you apart; I appointed you a prophet to the nations." When I almost died from my injury in 1999, it gave me a whole new outlook on life. I finally understood just how precious and fragile life really is. I can never put into words just how joyful I am just to be able to be here writing this to encourage you all.

In the Bible in the book of Mark when the disciples and Jesus got into the boat, Jesus said to them, "Let us cross over to the other side." Let that be a little whisper to you in your own journey with God. Even though there might be trouble and obstacles in your way you will cross over and get to the other side eventually.

Just as I started preparing this book for publication, I had a setback in my life. It was on Friday the 13th, of all days. After dinner I was letting my dog outside and fell and broke my ankle in three place. It all happened so fast I barely remember the details, but it was so painful that I knew there was some serious damage. My mom called 911 and a few minutes later three paramedics were carrying me to an ambulance. I was in the hospital for two weeks, and at first it seemed that there was so much damage that I might not walk again. Of course, I'd heard that before! Thanks to the work of Doctor James Bowers and some steel rods in my leg, I'll soon start working on walking with a walker.

During this recent stay in the hospital, I made a point of waking early, before the nurse would come at 6:00 to start the day. I wanted to make sure to have some time for myself and God. Though I was sometimes tempted to stay up late watching television, I knew that my body needed rest and that I needed time with

God if I was going to heal properly. As it says in 1 Corinthians, our bodies are the temple of the holy spirit. Take care of what God gave you!

This has been a rough setback, and at times I feel down about it. But then I think of Chesley "Sully" Sullenberger, the airline captain who successfully landed a disabled airplane carrying 155 passengers on the Hudson River. When reporters interviewed those passengers, many of them said that although they had been alive before the near crash, since coming so close to death they feel more alive than ever. That's how I feel -- I am more alive than ever before. I look at everything differently -- sunsets, eating, breathing and, especially, walking. I believe that his has all happened to bring a greater ending. I don't know what my ending will be, but I know it will exceed all that I can hope for.

Maybe you've experienced a trial that you feel only you can understand. That's how it is with me and my broken ankle. Of course, I wish that it didn't happen, but I believe that God's plan is for something good to come out of it. I don't know what that good might be, but it's not my job to figure it out. God is the driver and I am the passenger.

I wonder, of course, why I must endure the pain of not being able to walk all over again. The bible tells us that God's ways are not our ways nor his thoughts our thoughts. Maybe God wants to show me how much stronger I am now that I was in 1999. When I look back on the trials I have faced I see that the devil has tried to kill me three times: First, when I was born prematurely, then at the hands of my abusive ex-boyfriend, and finally when I was shot in the head. The devil must have thought the third time would be the charm, but he was wrong. James 1:12 tells us that blessed is the man who perseveres under trial because when he has stood the test he will receive the crown of life that God has promised to those who love him. I love the Lord with all my heart and I can never say thank you enough to him for sparing my life on June 11, 1999. I can't even begin to fathom the great things God has ahead for me but I just know it will be more than I could ever ask or hope for.

I may have come to the end of this physical story, but my spiritual story has just begun. I will leave you with this saying from Matthew: "With God, all things are possible." Always be encouraged in the Lord. I wish you the very best in life. God bless you all, and thank you for taking the time to read my story.